a

CONVERSION

THE JAMES SPRUNT LECTURES

In 1911, Mr. James Sprunt of Wilmington, North Carolina, established a perpetual lectureship at Union Theological Seminary in Virginia, which would enable the institution to secure from time to time the services of distinguished ministers and authoritative scholars as special lecturers on subjects connected with various departments of Christian thought and Christian work. The lecturers are chosen by the Faculty of the Seminary and a Committee of the Board of Trustees, and the lectures are published after their delivery in accordance with a contract between the lecturer and these representatives of the institution. The series of lectures on this foundation for the year 1931 is presented in this volume.

B. R. LACY, JR.,
President.

Union Theological Seminary
in Virginia.

CONVERSION

BY

W. P. PATERSON, D.D., LL.D.

PROFESSOR EMERITUS OF DIVINITY IN THE
UNIVERSITY OF EDINBURGH

With a Foreword by

PRINCIPAL W. A. CURTIS, D.D.

LONDON

HODDER AND STOUGHTON

First published . . *1939*

Made and Printed in Great Britain for HODDER AND STOUGHTON LTD.
by T. AND A. CONSTABLE LTD., Printers, Edinburgh

FOREWORD

To the theme of this book, the legacy of a vanished hand, the revered author had given years of reading and reflection. On it he had lectured in public and in the class-room. When leisure came to him, all too brief, from the labours of his strenuous and memorable life as teacher, public speaker and churchman, he turned upon it the energies of heart and intellect which age had touched so lightly. And the last evening granted to him found him engaged in the revision of the closing chapters.

To readers who were privileged to call him friend these pages will recall the tones and cadences of a voice born and trained to eloquence, the poise and reach of a questing mind whose critical acumen was singularly tempered by sympathy and tolerance. In writing, as in intercourse, he was an embodiment of the charity which even in controversy is forbearing and kind, thinking no evil, rejoicing in the truth, always aware that we know but in part and that only in part we can prophesy. In this study of what he called 'the remaking of souls,' given to a world in dire need of regeneration, there are evidenced the same fascination before the pageant of history, the same respect for the natural variety of religious thought and experience, and the same unshaken loyalty to evangelical faith, which characterised his *Rule of Faith* and *Nature of Religion*.

Acknowledgment is due to the Rev. D. Stuart Hopkirk, B.D., B.Litt., his pupil and his minister, whose scholarly help he had bespoken, for the final preparation of the manuscript for the press, and to Miss Elizabeth C. Paterson, M.A., his daughter, who, with Mr. John Sanderson, gave unstinted assistance in the work.

WILLIAM A. CURTIS.

EDINBURGH.

CONTENTS

INTRODUCTION

CHAPTER I

PRE-CHRISTIAN CONVERSION

CHAPTER II

IN THE MINISTRY OF JESUS

CONTENTS

CHAPTER III

IN THE PRIMITIVE CHURCH

CHAPTER IV

THE CATHOLIC SCHEME

CHAPTER V

THE EVANGELICAL SCHEME

CONTENTS

CHAPTER VI

PHILOSOPHICAL APPRAISEMENT

CHAPTER VII

THE SCIENTIFIC INVESTIGATION

CHAPTER VIII

THE RECENT SITUATION

INTRODUCTION

It is one of the paradoxes of Christianity that it attracts human nature by the offer of blessings which it highly values, while it repels it by criticism which deeply wounds its pride. Our religion had much to offer to man which was warmly welcomed. He has an instinctive dread of death and of the possibilities of a hereafter, and it went far to commend the Christian faith to the ancient world, and to keep it alive in the modern world, that it proclaimed a risen Saviour, and promised to believers a Heaven of perfected and enduring bliss. Again, man is naturally a religious being who desires to be in right relations with the God whom he worships, and the Christian Gospel gave an assurance of the forgiveness, on merciful terms, of the sins which provoke the divine anger. He is, further, a social being who shares of necessity in the common life of the family and the community, and by preference in the fellowship of various artificial groups; and the Christian Church made a unique appeal as the Society which gave a vision of a higher world, while it also fostered the nobler impulses, and guided them into various forms of spiritual and philanthropic service. Finally, Christianity cast a spell on the general mind as a philosophy suited to its apprehension which, surveying existence as a whole, gave credible assurance to the question as to the nature of the Supreme Being, the relation of the world to God, and the meaning and value of human life. The offence to the natural man was that Christianity declared his spiritual condition to be so unsatisfactory that he needs to undergo a radical change, and to be animated by a new spirit, with which he finds his chief joy in things which previously had little interested him, and becomes indifferent to other things on which he had set the highest store. In short, the message to man as man was that which is compressed in the saying to Nicodemus, 'Marvel not that I said unto thee, Ye must be born anew' (John iii. 7).

Human nature is also a paradox; for it is a strange blend of self-regarding instincts with self-denying affections and loyalties. The first are conspicuously dominant in the nations of the earth, which in their relations with one another might be described as associations for self-aggrandisement; and the second are seen at their best in the life of the family. In individuals the elements are mixed in such varying proportions that every combination is met with, ranging from a high grade of excellence to shameful depths of immorality and impiety. There is, at the same time, a representative of average human nature who is on the whole a self-centred being, habitually bent on getting out of life the most that he can of pleasure, possessions and honour, while his egotism is materially tempered and restrained by love of home and friends and country, by reverence for indubitable superiors, by respect for the laws and for public opinion, and by the elementary dictates of reason and conscience. This type may be regarded as a natural product, inasmuch as the self-seeking was bound up with the struggle for existence, the domestic affections were required for the preservation of the species, and the morality was part of the price exacted for sharing in the advantages of tribal and national life. Down to modern times rulers and legislators have been satisfied when the main body of citizens conformed to this standard of respectability, and have felt that the only action called for in the name of society was to punish, and possibly reform, those who did serious injury to others in body and estate, and to do what education can do to foster the good qualities in the rising generation. In the old world, however, and even before the Christian era, doubts arose as to whether the man, even if a useful self-centred and honoured citizen, was alive to the meaning of life and directed his energies to the attainment of the most valuable results. In India great religions arose which suggested, and had no small success in producing, a type of humanity in which the process of unselfing the individual was carried to an extraordinary pitch; while the Graeco-Roman world was stirred by Mystery Religions which proclaimed the necessity of a regeneration of some sort. We shall begin this study (Chapter I) with a brief account and estimate of these anticipations of Christian conversion.

Christianity undertook to fulfil the task of the remaking of souls in accordance with a higher pattern. In meditating on the question, 'Why did God become man?', Theology has given various reasons with more or less support from Scripture; but there is a growing and well-justified inclination to accept, at least in principle, the view expounded by Athanasius in his treatise on the Incarnation, viz. that the Son of God took human nature to the end that man might become a partaker in the divine nature. Unquestionably it was the purpose of Jesus, and that to which His ministry was mainly devoted, to create a new type of human being whose chief characteristic would be the overthrow of the domination of the worldly-minded and pleasure-loving self, and its replacement by the impulses of filial love of God and of fraternal love of man. We shall make a detailed study (Chapter II) of the ideal which was set forth by Jesus in His teaching, and exemplified in His own character and life, and also of the methods which He employed in the calling and the subsequent training of disciples.

The primitive Church had a deep sense of this aspect of the mission of Jesus. To Paul the work of Christ seemed so truly epoch-making that he gave Him the name of the second Adam: like to the first in that He impressed His image on a later race that derived life from Him; unlike in that, while the descendants of the first Adam were carnal and mortal, those who sprang from the second inherited a spiritual nature over which death had no power (1 Cor. xv. 45 ff.; Rom. v. 12 ff.). 'If any man is in Christ,' he summed up, 'he is a new creature' (2 Cor. v. 17). In the epistle bearing the name of the Lord's brother, Christians were bidden to think of themselves as the firstfruits of a new creative work accomplished by God through His word (James i. 18). And the theory of

a new phase of creation was borne out by the results
of the work of the apostolic Church. Our special
concern will be (Chapter III) with the apostolic
message which proved so effective, and with the
mysterious force, then at its strongest, which was
described as a baptism with the Holy Ghost and with
fire.

The Catholic Church, which developed out of the
primitive Church, became popular and prosperous,
and the spiritual guide of a world-wide Empire; and
it was a serious question whether and how far it would
be able to discharge its primary duty in the conversion
and sanctification of souls. There had been failure
as well as success even when its congregations were
small and select groups of persons who had consciously
and deliberately broken with the corruptions of the
world, and the Church might well be thought to be
charged with an impossible task when it was made
responsible for the Christian standing of vast masses
in many lands whose understanding of the Christian
ideal, as of the Christian faith, was of the slightest,
and in whom there continued to work a powerful
leaven of pagan superstition and immorality. In such
a situation there was a strong temptation to find a
substitute in something easier which at the same time
was of sufficient importance to satisfy the conscience;
and alternatives were found in the tasks of the development of Christian doctrine and its defence against
heretics, the improvement of ecclesiastical machinery
with the promotion of ecclesiastical interests, and the
building of churches to the glory of God such as
could 'dissolve men's souls in ecstasies, and bring all

Heaven before their eyes.' The Church, however, might not forget, and on occasion solemnly reaffirmed, that sinners of mankind need to be regenerated and to go on to fulfil the will of God in their sanctification. And a way was found which made it possible to think that the Church was effectively grappling with the most difficult work in the world. As regards the first stage—the making of a beginning in the new life—it was held that this had already taken place in the case of those, including infants, who had been baptized in the name of the Father and of the Son and of the Holy Ghost, and who had not by unbelief or evil purpose frustrated the efficacy of the means of grace. As to the second stage, in which the renewed soul went on towards the goal, the ideal was made more practicable by dividing Christians into two classes, and assigning to them a lower and a higher standard of character and conduct respectively. The great mass of the faithful had to remain in the world, and give themselves to the work of the home and the calling, and in their case the requirement was that they should be obedient children of Mother Church, seek the additional supplies of grace supplied through the Eucharist and the rest of the seven sacraments, practise the virtues of temperance, justice and charity, and refrain from the heinous sins which involved mortal penalties. On the other hand, the privilege was given to a small class, consisting along with the clergy of monks and nuns, of adopting a mode of life and a discipline that gave them the opportunity of rising to the highest plane of sanctity. In Chapter IV we deal more fully with this system, which, whatever

its faults of omission and of commission, must rank
as a remarkable attempt to carry out the Christian
programme subject to a realistic recognition of the
difficulty of the conditions under which the Church's
commission had to be carried out.

The Reformation was a complex movement in
which various religious motives, and also some mun-
dane motives, supplied the driving force, but it was
at least a chief purpose of the spiritual leaders to take
more effective measures to secure that those who
professed themselves Christians would be veritable
new creatures. In this interest they challenged the
Roman Catholic doctrine that a radical change took
place when baptism was administered to those offering no resistance. It was granted, and indeed
emphasised, that baptism is a signal means of grace,
but it was denied that the decisive change was
effected before the stage at which a personal decision
was possible, and the general view was that the means
by which the change is ordinarily brought about is
the reading, and especially the preaching, of the
Word of God. The only other ordinance recognised
as a sacrament was the Lord's Supper, and the condition of its efficacy was held to be the energising of
the faith which lays hold on Christ and claims the
blessings of the Christian salvation. Protestants also
repudiated the theory of a twofold standard of sanctity—holding that the confining of the highest ideal
to a class was wrong in principle, and also discredited
by monastic shortcomings and scandals, while it was
claimed that Christian men and women who take
their share in the necessary work of the world, and in

the continuation and education of the species, may attain with the help of the grace of God to the highest levels of the spiritual life. In Chapter V, we shall examine these positions, and inquire to what extent the substitution of a single for a double standard for all classes of Christians has been justified by Protestant experience.

In Chapter VI we shall inquire what Philosophy, and in Chapter VII what Psychology, has made of the subject of conversion. Theoretically, the task of Psychology is to describe the experience and to ascertain its proximate causes, while it falls to Philosophy to pronounce on the value of the experience, and to judge whether the causal explanation offered by the scientific discipline includes all causes. In practice, however, these limits have not been observed, as philosophers have taken a hand in the psychological investigation, while psychologists have gone on to speculate or to dogmatise in the capacity of philosophers. The value of conversion was necessarily considered by Philosophy, for one of its branches is Moral Philosophy, and as it is axiomatic for Moral Philosophy that the character of the good man is the most valuable thing in the world, it was bound to consider the claim of Christianity to produce a new and higher type of humanity. Philosophical opinion, however, has varied as to whether it could adopt the doctrine of conversion. There was inherited from Greece an ideal of goodness which includes the virtues of prudence, courage, temperance and justice, along with the spirit of piety, and the general opinion was that this was adequate, with additions from the

Christian programme which were comprehended in benevolence. But there have also been philosophers who held that nothing less than a conversion is called for—among them Kant, who declared that the governing maxims of the ordinary man need to be replaced by self-effacing loyalty to the moral law, and Hegel, who found the quintessence of the moral law in the principle that a man must die that he may live.

In recent times the importance of conversion was rediscovered by Psychology. The subject had fallen into the background in the teaching of the later Protestant pulpit, and the message of the new birth had been left to minor sects and to unofficial evangelists, when it was again made popular by the American School of Psychology, and in particular by William James's study of the varieties of religious experience. The contribution consisted of an analysis of the experience of professed converts, a distinction of types of conversion, and a genetic explanation within scientific limits of the spiritual phenomena. Grounds will be given for thinking that the value of this work as a scientific contribution has been somewhat overestimated; and, further, that when all has been found out that can be found out about second causes, there is still good reason to recognise God as the first cause, and also to hold to a belief in the additional factor that has been known since the apostolic age as the grace of God.

In our distracted and disillusioned age it has become increasingly evident that the call to conversion is an urgent duty of the Church. Even the secular

mind has realised that the nations need the gift of a
new heart if they are not to head for unexampled
strife and tragedy, and it is not beyond reasonable
hope that there may be a growth of the sense of
brotherhood which will at least be a counterpoise to
their ingrained egotism. There are also large classes
whose need is manifest; one consisting of those who
are called to faith that they may cease to feel themselves alone and defenceless in a menacing and cruel
world, another of those who are called to repentance
that they may find the rest of soul which they have
failed to find in the pursuit of pleasure or of worldly
goods. That there is a growing perception of the
deep-seated nature of the evil is evidenced by the
widespread disposition to make trial of fresh spiritual
ventures, whether of faith, superstition or unbelief,
and not least by the fact that the movements which
in recent days have evoked most response throughout
the Protestant world have presupposed the deep distress of the natural man and renewed the promise of
an enduement of power from on high. In former
periods the Church successfully coped with a similar
situation—notably in the early Roman Empire, at
the Renaissance, and in the period of the French
Revolution—and the major question to which an
historical study leads up is whether the latter-day
Church is equipped for repeating the spiritual success
of former days. One condition is that it should still
hold the substance of the message which in the earlier
periods proved effectual in quickening souls into
newness of life, and that it should arrange extended
opportunities for making this message known to the

multitudes who, even in Christian lands, are ignorant of the inward blessing that is offered in the Gospel. The other condition is that the Christian congregation should again be known to the world as a school of character in which all recognise that they are enrolled to believe that, whatever their present shortcomings, they may go on to become selfless as Jesus was selfless, and to take their share in continuing His self-sacrificing mission to the world (Chapter VIII).

CHAPTER I

PRE-CHRISTIAN CONVERSION

IN the natural man the elements are strangely mixed. Theology teaches that he is a corrupt being with a habitual bias to sin, and Psychology pictures him as driven and tossed by appetites and passions, with self-gratification for his guiding-star. The chief matter in dispute is whether this evil condition is the punishment of a primeval fall or the inheritance from an animal ancestry. He has also a higher nature in which faith sees lineaments of the divine image, and which for Philosophy is at least the custodian of the crowning values of truth and beauty, virtue and piety. But on the whole the lower nature is dominant, and the typical man may be defined as a self-centred creature held in check in some degree by heart and conscience and by social pressure. It has therefore been a standing problem how the best was to be made of the unstable, difficult and dangerous subject. And there have been two methods of treatment which may be distinguished as the way of amendment and the way of conversion.

The usual course has been to seek to improve the human being without seriously disturbing his natural centre of gravity. Rulers and parents have ever been concerned to give some training to the rising generation in what were deemed good customs and maxims, and with the progress of civilisation their efforts were

A

reinforced by ethically minded priests and sages. Great service in this kind was rendered to China by Confucius. The moral philosophers of ancient Greece set up a standard of prudence, temperance, courage and justice which, while high-pitched, was based on observation and illustrated from common life, and was thus within the compass of man as man. Socrates relied on growth in knowledge for the amendment of character, while Aristotle insisted that, as in the case of arts and crafts, it is corresponding practice that makes for perfection. It may, however, be noted that the Platonic Socrates came to the conclusion that, even if virtue can be taught, efficient teachers were not available, while pre-eminent goodness was interpreted by him as an incalculable gift of God.[1]

The more heroic policy, initiated by great religions, aimed at a radical transformation of the natural man. Instead of repairing and extending the house it was proposed to rebuild it according to a different ground-plan. Otherwise put, a revolution was planned in the kingdom of the soul, when self was to be deposed and a greater would reign in its stead. There were, however, two different conceptions as to how the throne ought to be filled. One school, which may be termed the theocentric, asserted the sovereign rights of God, and sought to change the self-seeking creature into an intimate and instrument of the most High. The other, which may be termed the nomocentric, sought to capture the soul by the constraining power of a lofty moral ideal. These were successively represented in India by Brahmanism and Buddhism, and in the

[1] *Dialogue of Meno*, 99-100.

Hellenistic world by Mystery-religions and Stoicism. The religion of Israel, while essentially theocentric, effected a certain synthesis of the two systems.

I

THE INDIAN TYPES

In the Vedic period religious authorities were chiefly concerned with the proper observance of sacrificial rites, and their ethical efforts were limited to putting some restraint on the lusts of the natural man. The aim of Brahmanism was to change him by contemplation and asceticism into a God-possessed and even God-intoxicated creature. Buddhism sought to produce a new man by enlightening him as to the meaning or meaninglessness of existence, and giving him to feel the spell of a self-abnegating mode of life.

1. The God for whom Brahmanism claimed the dominion over the soul was a mighty and mysterious being, nearer than breathing and also more distant than the stars. 'The intelligent, whose body is spirit, whose form is light,' it was written, 'whose thoughts are true, whose nature is like ether (omnipresent and invisible), from whom all works, all desires, all sweet odours and tastes proceed, he who embraces all this, he is my self within the heart, smaller than a corn of rice, also greater than the earth, greater than the sky, greater than heaven, greater than all these worlds.' [1] 'That which is that subtle essence,' a father instructed his son, 'in it all that exists has its self. It

[1] *The Sacred Books of the East*, 1900, vol. i.: Khandogya-upanishad, iii. 14, 2 ff.

is the True. It is the Self, and thou art it.'[1] There were indeed diverse interpretations of the dogma 'That art thou.' It meant for one that he was identical with God, for another that he was part of the all which is God, for a third that he was a manifestation of His presence and power. But at least it was common ground that man's chief end is to realise a vital union with the Supreme Being. And this led to contempt for the lesser goods which the world has to offer. Of Brahmanas who 'know that Self' it was said that they 'have risen above the desire for sons, wealth and (new) worlds.'[2] To them a stone, a son and gold are alike. One who is abstinent may still have a desire for the objects of sense, but 'even the taste for them departs from one when he has seen the Supreme.'[3]

In the religious legislation the life of the males of the higher castes was organised as a progressive course that led up to absorption in God and the complete suppression of the self-seeking spirit. The youth of the favoured classes were early dedicated to a higher life, and invested with the sacred cord. Their education was largely a training in piety and virtue. Prayer, the repetition of the name, and the inward recitation of texts were enjoined, and much stress was laid on self-control, described as 'restraining his organs, which run wild among alluring sensual objects, like a charioteer his horses.'[4] In early manhood the pupil went on to the stage of the householder when

[1] *The Sacred Books of the East*, 1900, vol. i. : Khandogya-upanishad, vi. 9, 4.

[2] *S.B.E.*, vol. xv.: Brihadaranyaka-upanishad, iii. 5, 1.

[3] *Ibid.*, vol. viii.: Bhagavadgita, chap. ii.

[4] *Ibid.*, vol. xxv.: 'Laws of Manu,' ii. 82 ff.

the commandments were: 'do not neglect the study
of the Veda, do not cut off the line of children, do not
swerve from the truth; do not swerve from duty, do
not neglect what is useful, do not neglect greatness.' [1]
The work to which one was born he was forbidden
to forsake, for at this stage a secular calling was held
to be liberating rather than fettering—'always perform without attachment the work that thou hast to
do, for thus one attains to the Supreme.' [2] A means
of subsistence was to be found which either causes no
or little pain to others, and one was to be satisfied
with earnings coming spontaneously, free from all
animosity, and equable in success or ill-success.[3]
When a man had thus discharged his obligations to
society, and came in sight of the inevitable close, he
was bidden to flee from the world to the forest, where
he joined a hermit-community and sought a greater
religious experience in the contemplative life of an
ascetic. The exercises of the Yoga discipline, especially 'the restraint of the life-breaths,' were used to
assist meditation, or to induce a hypnotic state that
invited an influx of light and joy. 'By ascetic penance,' it was said, 'goodness is obtained, from goodness understanding is reached, from understanding
the Self is obtained, and he who has obtained that
does not return.' [4] The promise annexed was that
those who thus found God need have no fear of repeating the trials and humiliations of a similar existence. They were no longer under the law that 'as a

---

[1] *S.B.E.*, vol. xv.: Taittiriyaka-upanishad, i. 11, 1.
[2] *Ibid.*, vol. viii.: Bhagavadgita, chap. iii.
[3] *Ibid.*, vol. xxv.: 'Laws of Manu,' iv. 2 ff.
[4] *Ibid.*, vol. xv.: Maitrayana-upanishad, iv. 3.

man, casting off old clothes, puts on others and new ones, so the embodied (self) casting off old bodies, goes to others and new ones.'[1] A modern sketch of the emancipated saint may be reproduced. 'He sits in meditation, his body in repose, his breathing deep and regulated. Glancing back on the world he has left behind he beholds it as a vast jungle of life and death, with whirling clouds of smoke given off from the fire of the Infinite Being. Thence his thoughts turn to objects that speak more plainly of the Infinite —a white fleece, a lotus-flower, a flash of lightning, but chiefly the person that is revealed in the human eye. He also approaches the Highest through the ideas of truth and joy or of the beloved, feels Him in the warmth of his body, and hears Him in the holy syllable Om. Then he ceases to be conscious of anything finite, even his own perceiving mind. The ego no longer lives: in it lives the Being that no form encloses and no formula limits. The Infinite stands before him unveiled, or rather he is merged in the Infinite. That art thou.'[2]

The pessimistic strain in Brahmanism may be partly explained by the mentality of old age. It reflected the feelings of one who, when he looks back on the labours of a lifetime, suspects that they were not worth while, and is disposed to think that those were the more fortunate who found a short-cut to the grave. The time comes when the worker must make way for one of a younger generation, and it is a noble conception that in the remaining years the mind should

[1] *S.B.E.*, vol. viii.: Bhagavadgita, chap. ii. 3.
[2] Oldenberg, *Die Lehre der Upanishaden*, p. 141 (condensed).

be filled with thoughts of truth, beauty and goodness, and rise above the realm of change and decay to the presence of Him who is the same yesterday, to-day and for ever. It compares very favourably with a prevalent view that the chief problem of old age is how to kill time, and that it is best solved by being a good sleeper, reading the lightest of fiction, and playing such games as are still possible to the failing powers. But the Brahmanical programme was unnecessarily harsh, while many found themselves in the case of the king of whom we read that, after long trial of the life in the forest, he implored a passing saint to inform him why he had missed the goal. The recluse might also reproach himself for sinning against love when he dragged an aged helpmeet with him into the wilderness and ceased to concern himself with the welfare of children and children's children.

The disparaging estimate of the world and its activities spread from venerated teachers to ardent pupils, and in the post-Vedic period there was a growing company of aspirants that shirked or curtailed the duties of the householder. And respect is due to those who in mid-career renounced for a spiritual ideal all that the world had given or promised them. If they buried their talents, and made no return for their upbringing, they had at least a better defence than those in the modern Western world who live pleasure-seeking and useless lives because they have been amply provided for by the laws of inheritance or by early good fortune in business. And some found a second vocation in the capacity of the teacher or other helper of toiling humanity. But when this was not done the premature flight from the life of action was contrary to duty, and it was also inconsistent with their belief that the human self is a manifestation of God, since nothing is more certain than that the power adored as the Infinite is a ceaseless and tireless worker in the universe of space and time.

The Brahmanical scheme of regeneration was founded on the truth that the new creature should be rooted in God and nourished by His life. The drawback was that its God was the impersonal Absolute, and as such did not possess the moral attributes that are essential to a true communion with His children. Moreover, the pantheistic doctrine implied that all that a man does is in the last resort the doing of God, and the practical effect was to weaken if not suppress the sense of sin, and to detach piety from zeal for righteousness. Nor did morality get support from all the lesser divinities whom the people were encouraged to worship as symbols of the Highest. No doubt there was much sound moral teaching in the religious law-book bearing the name of Manu, but this was inspired by good sense and the social conscience rather than by the religious creed. The finding of an impartial expositor is that 'the total impression made by the Upanishads is that of an intellectual exercise which aimed at the attainment, partly of immediate goods, partly of the highest good, . . . and there is no attempt to make the theoretical philosophy a ground of morality.' [1]

2. Buddhism reaffirmed the necessity of a second

[1] Berriedale Keith, *Religion and Philosophy of the Veda and Upanishads*, 1925, p. 584.

birth, but gave to it a purely human content, and relied on enlightenment and self-effort to effect the change. The prototype of the new experience was that of an Indian prince who was a young man when the Jews were delivered from the Babylonian captivity, and who died about the time that Greece was saved at the battle of Salamis. Gautama reached the status of the householder, was initiated into the business and tasted of the pleasures of a court, married and begat a son, and then escaped to the wilderness to seek the rest of soul that was promised there to the seeker after God. Dissatisfied with the results of asceticism, he proceeded to think out the human situation for himself, and illumination came as he meditated under the bo-tree. The sum of it was that he diagnosed the universal human malady, believed that he discovered the cause, and prescribed the corresponding remedy. The next forty years were given to preaching and the training of converts, and the harvest from his labours was the rise of a faith which ranks as one of the three universal religions.

The Buddha sought to compass the death of the natural man, and even to rend him in pieces. The first step was to excite his disgust with the conditions in which he finds himself alive. Earth was depicted as a place of torment—'birth is painful, decay is painful, disease is painful, death is painful, union with the unpleasant is painful, painful is separation from the pleasant, and any craving that is unsatisfied that too is painful.' The next was to explain why he is in this miserable plight. 'The origin of suffering,' it was taught, 'is that thirst (or craving) accompanied by sensual delight, seeking satisfaction now here now there—that is to say the craving for the gratification of the passions, or the craving for (a future) life, or a craving for success (in this present life).' The remedy, so ran the third truth, 'is the destruction, in which no passion remains, of this very thirst; the laying aside of, the getting rid of, the being free from, the harbouring no longer of this thirst.' [1] The disciple was bidden to 'cut down, not one tree only, but the whole forest and its undergrowth.' [2] The clinging to life or the desire of self-preservation, this was identified as the ultimate cause of the tragedy of the human lot.

The 'noble truths' of the misery of man and its cause were professedly reached by an objective study of human life, and were thus akin to the inductions and causal explanations that are now offered in the name of Anthropology and Sociology. But the procedure fell far short of the scientific standard. The thesis that human existence is essentially a state of suffering rests on an arbitrary selection from the facts, as was admitted by the disciple who said that 'as many kinds of wreaths can be made from a heap of flowers, so many good things may be achieved by a mortal when once he is born.' [3] And when desire was said to be the cause of the misery of the human lot it was justly objected by Mara the adversary that 'he who has sons has delight in sons, he who has cows has delight likewise in cows; for substance is the delight of man, but he who has no substance has no delight.' [4]

[1] S.B.E., vol. xi.: Dhamma-kakka-ppavattana-Sutta, 5-7.
[2] Ibid., vol x.: Dhammapada, chap. xx. 283.
[3] Ibid., vol. x.: Dhammapada, chap. iv. 53.
[4] Ibid., vol. x.: Dhaniyasutta, 15.

He ignored the vital distinction, which conscience insists on drawing, between evil and good desires. We should certainly cease to suffer if we ceased to have the will to live and to desire the means, but on the whole reason has emphatically agreed with instinct that in that event the loss would far outweigh the gain. The findings should have been limited to the propositions that suffering is a large and grim part of human experience, that a chief cause is the selfishness which seeks pleasure and advantage without regard to conflicting claims of God and man, and that the best defence against unhappiness is to make one's chief end a purpose of service that relegates self to the lowest room.

The means prescribed for the extinction of desire was the cultivation of 'right views, right aspirations, right speech, right conduct, right livelihood, right effort, right mindfulness or inclination and right contemplation.' [1] What this meant was made clearer in the description of the aims and means at the successive stages of the ascent out of the depths. The first step was conversion in the sense of the beginning of the new life, and this resulted from faith in Buddha and acceptance of his teaching. At the second stage the believer bridled the lusts of the flesh and subdued the passions of hatred and revenge. At the third he was freed from all doubt, from heresy, and from all unkindness and vexation of spirit. Having thus broken the chains that bound him to earth, he had good hope that his present incarnation would be the last and that Nirvana was at hand.

[1] *S.B.E.*, vol. xi.: Dhamma-kakka-ppavattana-Sutta, 8.

The converts fell into two classes—those who fled from the world to a monastic life, when they had the prospect of a speedy release, and those who, abiding in home and calling, bore a lighter yoke though at the price of a prolongation of misery. Yet the ideal of the layman still rose high above the conventional moral code. Among the greatest blessings he was bidden to reckon these: 'to succour father and mother, to cherish wife and child, to follow a peaceful calling; to give alms, and live righteously, to help one's relatives and do blameless deeds; to cease and abstain from sin, to eschew strong drink, not to be weary in well-doing; reverence and lowliness, contentment and gratitude, the regular hearing of the law, to be long-suffering and meek, to associate with the order of mendicants, religious talk at due seasons, temperance and chastity, a conviction of the four great truths, the hope of Nirvana, a mind unshaken by the things of the world, without anguish or passion, and secure.'[1] As to the nature of the promised Nirvana, opinion has differed both in ancient and modern times. The probable view, supported by Buddha's conception of the soul as an attribute not a substance, is that he believed it would finally go out like a lamp that has used up its oil. But this doctrine was too strong meat for babes, and converts were enjoined to give their whole mind in the first period to subduing their lusts and showing loving-kindness, leaving over speculation on transcendental subjects until their wisdom was matured by self-denial.

The Buddhistic model of the new creature was

[1] Rhys Davids, Art. 'Buddhism,' *Ency. Brit.*, 9.

defective on the positive side. The natural man has shown marvellous courage and energy in grappling with the hard conditions of life on our planet, and he may well be thought more admirable than a type of new man who shirks the tasks prescribed by the situation, and comes to find comfort in the hope of a sleep from which there will be no awakening. Moreover, man as man has a religious nature which adds to his dignity and enriches his inner life, and it was foolish to think to reach the highest level by ignoring the Power that created him and set his feet in the way to the goal. That the irreligion of Buddhism was a fatal blemish was the considered judgment of the peoples of India, who generally rejected it in favour of cults that offered some form of a divine friendship. But against these defects is to be set the great work which it did as a school of sympathy and self-sacrifice. If in theory the chief concern of the enlightened Buddhist was to expedite his escape from conscious existence, he had a fellow-feeling that drew him back to service on the world of labour and sorrow, even as it was related of the founder that when he had earned release he voluntarily returned to earth to be the saviour of his brethren. The signal achievement was that he persuaded a large section of the human race to subscribe to a moral ideal in which brotherly love and the passive virtues were given the place of honour, and that in every generation following there has been a multitude of disciples who translated the self-renouncing programme into life and deed.

II

Graeco-Roman Types

While these movements were in progress in India, Greece was stirred by a religious revival in which ventures were made on the same lines as in the Oriental faiths. Something was derived from India, for ideas like seeds readily find carriers to distant soils, but on the whole the coincidence was due to a spiritual quickening which stirred the chief nurseries of civilisation as well as Palestine in the course of the millennium preceding our era.

1. The theocentric scheme of Brahmanism had a parallel in the Mystery Religions which spread through the Hellenistic world, and which in the later centuries had an important supplement in Neoplatonic mysticism.

The Mystery cults sprang from rude agrarian rites, which were gradually purified and enriched in the interests of a progressive culture. What they proposed and achieved in their highest development has been much debated. The opinion of the primitive Church was that 'nothing was done that was profitable for life and morals.' [1] In the eighteenth century it was a popular view that esoteric teaching was given which attacked pagan superstition, witnessed to the truth about God, the soul and immortality, and inculcated morality as the true service of God.[2] In the next phase the leading scholar maintained that 'nothing

---

[1] Lactantius, *Institutio*, iv. 3.
[2] Warburton, *Divine Legation*, 1837, ii. 4.

was heard amid the slaughter and the offerings save
a song of praise or a muttered vow,' and that there was
'no systematic propagation of truth.'[1] In the recent
period much has been written about the origin of the
Mysteries, with a preference for a totemistic explanation, while the judgment on the matured institution
has been friendly and sometimes enthusiastic. It has
been brought out that there was a marked distinction
between the State-cults as represented by the Eleusinian Mysteries, and the private cults as represented
at their best by the Orphic rites. The Eleusinian
festival was the joint-creation of religious leaders and
patriotic statesmen, and their common purpose would
be limited to doing something for the religious and
moral improvement of the citizens, and especially of
the adolescents. In Orphism a new birth was the goal
of the initiated, and souls were encouraged to wing
their way to the heights of the spiritual world.

'The Eleusinian Mysteries,' it is said, 'were the
paramount fact of the Attic state-religion, and their
administration the most complex function of the Attic
state-church.'[2] The festival was for ancient Athens
what Holy Week has been for a modern European
capital. After a year's probation, during which they
were admitted to the Lesser Mysteries, the candidates
assembled in a temple near the Acropolis to be
addressed by a hierophant. On the morrow they
went to the sea to bathe and sacrifice, two more days
were given to fasting and purification, and on the
evening of the third they marched in solemn pro-

---

[1] Lobeck, *Aglaophamus*, i. 2.
[2] Farnell, *The Cults of the Greek States*, iii. p. 127.

cession to Eleusis carrying an image of their patron-God. 'The *Mystae* were admitted to the holy building, the splendid illumination seemed dazzlingly bright after the darkness outside, the strange apparitions, the impressive voices, the gorgeous dresses of the actors, the magnificence of the sacred drama—all these they heard in awestruck silence. Then came the crowning act of the ceremony; they had perhaps before this drunk the sacred draught, they were admitted one by one to touch, to kiss the holy things, to lift them from the cist, to put them into the basket, to taste them, to replace them in the cist, and to pronounce the sacred formula.' [1]

The obvious purpose of this festival was to strengthen the belief in a future state of existence, and to give the hope of a blessed immortality. The theme of the original rites was the miracle of the seasons in which decay and death are followed by a rush of new life, and the staple of the sacred pantomime was the story of Demeter and Kore with the moral that there is a power stronger than death. It was assumed that there are two places prepared for the departed—a Hades whose terrors were summed up as darkness and filth, and an upper world of light and joy in the society of the Olympian gods. The awakening message was that the entrance to Heaven, and the only entrance, was by the gate of the Mysteries. 'Blessed among men upon the earth,' says Demeter in an ancient hymn, 'is he who has seen these things,' but he that is uninitiate in the rites and has no part in them has never an equal lot in the cold place of

---

[1] Ramsay, Art. 'Mysteries,' *Ency. Brit.*, 9.

darkness.[1] Sophocles spoke of this as the only way
of escape from future torment—

> O thrice-blessed they
> That ere they pass to Hades have beheld
> Those mysteries, for they only in that world
> Have life, the rest have utter misery.[2]

Had this initiation also value for character and conduct? The ancients, said Rohde, knew practically
nothing of a moral influence exercised by them, and
besides, the institution had no machinery for the
purpose. In this view he had the support of
Diogenes, who asked contemptuously 'if Pataecion
the thief was going to have a better lot after death
than Epaminondas just because he was initiated,' and
evidently did not think that when the thief was
initiated anything was done to ensure that he repented
and would mend his ways.[3] But the presumption is
that the Athenian State patronised the Eleusinian
institution as a means of raising the morale of the
community, which it certainly did not do if it left the
impression that in the eyes of gods conduct did not
matter. And that it supplied a moral dynamic is the
reasonable inference from the respectful and even
reverential language of a long line of philosophers,
poets and statesmen. Aristotle says that the festival
only moved the feelings, but this was no small service
if it enlisted the feelings, as he probably meant, on
the side of the things that were pure and honest and

---

[1] Homeric Hymn, Eng. Trans. Cornford, *Greek Religious Thought*,
1923, p. 51.
[2] Pearson, *The Fragments of Sophocles*, No. 837.
[3] *Psyche*, 1898, i. p. 312.

B

of good report. Aristophanes put on the stage a band of initiates, and evidently accepted their profession that they lived in pious fashion, and that among them such things were unknown as wronging strangers, ill-treating parents and swearing false oaths.[1] Three centuries later there was a weighty tribute from Cicero who, having himself trodden the path, wrote that he knew of nothing better as a guide to a rational and happy life with a good hope in death.[2] Doubtless initiation meant for many nothing more than a passport to Heaven, but there would at least be some who heard in the solemnities a call to a life in accordance with their highest ideals. And as there is evidence of Orphic influence in the place of honour given to Iacchus, it may be inferred that there were priests concerned with the institution who found in it the promise and the potency of a spiritual transformation both for themselves and for disciples.

The Orphic Mysteries came to be identified with the idea of a new birth. They 'led to a rejection of one's old life, and the entering on a new life, which is conversion.'[3] It was a case of the conversion of an institution, for the original was a rustic festival at which intoxication was taken for divine possession, while in the later period the coveted experience was spiritual ecstasy in union and communion with a divine being. The special object of worship was Dionysus, also called Zagreus, son of Zeus and Semele. The story was that when a little child he was ap-

---

[1] *The Frogs*, l. 456. (*Vide* Kennedy, *St. Paul and the Mystery Religions*, 1913, p. 84.)
[2] *De Legibus*, ii. 14.
[3] Nock, *Conversion, from Alexander the Great to Augustine*, p. 28.

proached by the Titans with a gift of toys, changed himself into a bull, and was slain, cooked and devoured.   Thereupon Zeus launched his thunderbolts and reduced the murderers to dust and ashes. He ate the heart of the child, which had been rescued by Athena, and restored him to life, while out of the remains of the Titans, with which those of the divine child had been mingled, he formed the human race.[1] It was a grotesque tale which may first have been applauded at a festival of the wine-god, but to the Orphic philosopher it became a parable that enshrined deep spiritual truths.   It could mean that man needs a salvation as he has a lower nature derived from the Titans, that he is capable of it as he has a divine nature derived from the offspring of Zeus, and that the way of salvation is to reinforce the divine elements by physical union with God.   The essential content, according to Miss Harrison, was that the worshipper became divine and immortality was the consequence.[2] As to the effect upon the initiates, the latest finding is that 'they had the sense of being endowed with a new essence which involved a moral transformation, and that they were more pious and just and in everything better than other people.'[3]   Plato was repelled by the religious frenzy of the movement, and pilloried its mendicant prophets who produce books written by Musaeus and Orpheus, and persuade not only individuals but whole cities that atonements for sin may be made by sacrifices and amusements that fill a

---

[1] Lobeck, *op. cit.*, ii. pars. ii. v. 28-35.
[2] *Prolegomena to the Study of Greek Religion*, 1908, Introduction, p. xi and p. 574.
[3] Macchioro, *From Orpheus to Paul*, p. 102.

vacant hour and redeem us from the pains of hell.[1] But from the literary remains it appears that there were teachers who had much the same vision of God as Plato himself, and for whom purification meant renewal in the likeness of the divinity whose nature and whose name is Love.

How character could be changed by a kindred Egyptian cult may be learned from the *Metamorphoses* of Apuleius, who lived in the first century of our era. Apart from the story of his hero being changed into an ass and changed back again, he gives an obviously authentic description of a religious and moral experience. Lucius hired a lodging within the precincts of a temple of Isis, when the goddess appeared to him in a dream, bade him live chastely and frugally, and promised him health of soul 'as by a certain kind of regeneration.' After a course of instruction, during which he neither ate flesh nor drank wine, he was clothed with a linen robe, and conducted to the most secret place of the temple for meditation and prayer. In the night watches his spirit went on a journey in which he beheld the gates of Hades and the glories of Heaven, and also worshipped the great gods. In the morning he came forth with a garland on his head and a torch in his hand, bowed before the image of the goddess, and went through initiatory rites that ended on the third day with a sacred meal. He vowed to the goddess that he would 'ever keep her close to his breast.' He paid a visit to his parents and friends, then proceeded to Rome, 'daily making his prayers to the sovereign goddess.' Isis gave him to know that

[1] *Republic*, Bk. ii. 364.

he would please her by diligence in his profession, and returning to the law-courts he 'executed his office in great joy with a shaven crown.'[1]

The attraction of the Mysteries was that they offered to devout souls an intimate divine friendship. The weakness was that the reputed divinities had very poor credentials, for their existence was more than doubtful, and when this was taken for granted they were ill-equipped to be the mediators of a true salvation. The wine-god, even when he had been transfigured, was an unsatisfactory witness to the moral ideal, and the Mithras whose worship spread widely in the later Roman Empire was a mythical Persian figure adapted to the taste of the Roman soldiery. Moreover it was difficult to feel sure, in the chaos of polytheistic beliefs, that the best choice had been made of a divine friend, and it could be thought prudent to connect oneself with a variety of cults. It is therefore not surprising that in course of time finer spirits left it to the multitude to find some comfort and edification in the questionable symbols, and themselves passed on to seek the Highest in the school of Neoplatonism.

It was presupposed by the Neoplatonist that man is by nature of such a dignity that his need is amendment rather than a radical conversion. His real self being divine, it was sufficient to cleanse it from the filth by which it is commonly clothed and concealed. The salvation he needs is that God should dwell in him, and that he should know himself one with God. 'The soul is in travail and longing,' wrote Plotinus, 'can we find a charm for this pain? God comes into

---

[1] Eng. Trans. *The Golden Ass*, Bk. xi. 28.

the house of him who invites him and gives him light. This is the life of Godlike and blessed men, a life that takes no pleasure in earthly things, a flight of the alone to the alone.'[1] And there was an ethical strain in this faith. As Dean Inge puts it, men were bidden not only to remember their origin in the Divine, but also to think of themselves as members of a spiritual community. But the same writer has made it clear that the statement is subject to important reservations, since the Divine who came to dwell in the saint was the impersonal Infinite, and there was none 'of that deep personal loyalty, none of that intimate dialogue between soul and soul, none of that passion of love . . . which are so prominent in later mystical literature.'[2] Nor may we read too much into the saying that the God-possessed knew themselves members one of another. It meant that they had sympathy with their fellow-men as one with themselves in divine origin and high vocation, but not that they agonised over their sins and sorrows, and were eager to bear their burdens. Among the beauties of the soul was reckoned an apathy that held the saint aloof from the distressful turmoil of the world. 'The call to seek and save that which was lost, the moral knight-errantry which "rides abroad redressing human wrongs," the settled purpose to confront . . . human society as it organises itself apart from God . . . with another association of "fellow-workers with God"— this call is but faintly heard by philosophers of this type, and they leave such work to others.'[3]

---

[1] Ennead v. 3, 17; VI. 9, 11.
[2] *The Philosophy of Plotinus*, ii. pp. 160 ff.   [3] Inge, *op. cit.* ii. p. 190.

2. In the same period there were ethical schools that won disciples by the attraction of a self-renouncing ideal.[1] The Cynics, led by Antisthenes and Diogenes, scorned the comforts and even the decencies of life, and taught that the true wealth is the riches laid up in the soul of the wise. If there were camp-followers who were repudiated as ribald beggars, the leaders were hailed as 'messengers sent from Zeus to show men how they had gone astray in their estimates of good and evil.'[2] One such was Dion of Prusa who had successfully followed the profession of a sophist, and also made a fortune in business by dubious methods, until he was brought to self-examination by a bread-riot in which he nearly lost his life. 'Then his old life seemed empty, and he became a travelling preacher exhorting men to virtue and preaching the Cynic creed—limit your needs, and look for happiness to yourself and not to the multitude of your possessions.'[3]

The school of the Stoics yielded the most convincing examples of a conversion wrought by a self-effacing ideal. Its product was a spiritual aristocrat who loyally accepted the duties of the human lot, faced its dangers with courage, and bore with dignity its sufferings and humiliations. There was also a vein of piety, exemplified by Posidonius and Marcus Aurelius, of which the note was reverent submission to the Power that was recognised as the soul and the law of the universe. They claimed to produce conversions of the most radical kind. 'They tell us,' said the doubting Plutarch, 'that a man may fall asleep

---

[1] Nock, *op. cit.*, chap. xi., 'Conversion to Philosophy.'
[2] Epictetus, *Discourses*, iii., κ. β'. 23.
[3] Livingstone, *The Mission of Greece*, p. 107.

mad and ignorant and unjust and unchaste, and a
slave forsooth and poor and needy, and rise up on the
same day having become a king and rich and prosperous and temperate and just and firm and free from
vain opinions.' [1] In Seneca's case it was a gradual
process, but the issue was a profound and enduring
change of character. The eloquent fact is that the
self-abnegating ideal of Stoicism was the refuge of
noble souls in an age when the spirit of the flesh and
of the world were revealed in all their power and
ugliness while the religion of the fathers was a spent
force, and doubtless its ideal of resignation coupled
with moral obligation is the highest to which men can
aspire when faith in the living God fails, and it seems
that an inflexible world-order is the ultimate reality
with which we have to do.

III

Old Testament Anticipations

It was from Israel, not from India or Greece, that
the spiritual leadership was to come. In the doctrine
of the one God, almighty, all-wise and all-good, the
foundation was truly laid for the work of regeneration.
The knowledge of the all-holy God produced a sense
of sin which made conversion appear a necessity, and
the knowledge of His goodness made it credible that
He willed to raise His creatures to higher dignity, and
enrich them with greater powers from on high. In

---

[1] 'Stoicos absurdiora poetis dicere.' Plutarch, *Moralia* (Bernardakis),
vi. p. 281.

this regard the impressive features of the Old Testament religion were the lofty types of conversion illustrated by prophets and psalmists, and the elaborate provision made under priestly rule for the training of a nation in godliness and righteousness.

1. The new man of the prophetic religion was a God-centred being. There were two varieties, of which one had more the character of the faithful servant, the other that of the grateful beneficiary of the King of Kings.

The religious consciousness of the prophets was dominated by a sense of dedication to the service of God. Their piety was indeed many-sided, and the fuller picture is that of 'holy men waiting for the salvation of God, deeply penetrated by the sense of sin, having no hope but in God's mercy, living by faith, and working in the strength of the Lord.' [1] But the man of God was above all the loyal servant whom his master summoned to receive his orders, and whose privilege it was to be used as mouthpiece and instrument in the conduct of his business. In the story of Moses at the burning bush the central incidents are the vision of God that brought the shepherd to his knees, and his final acceptance of the commission to deliver Israel out of the house of bondage (Exod. iii. 1 ff.). Isaiah was apprehended by a more splendid vision followed by a purging from sin, and when the Lord asked 'Whom shall I send?' the answer was 'Here am I, send me' (vi. 1 ff.). The prefatory Psalm gives it as distinctive of the righteous that 'his delight is in the law of the Lord; and in his law doth he

[1] A. B. Davidson, *Old Testament Prophecy*, 1903, p. 10.

meditate day and night' (Ps. i. 2). There were sweet
singers on whom the divine commandments had laid
a compulsion which was felt to be nothing less than
the power of God unto conversion—'the law of the
Lord is perfect, restoring the soul' (xix. 7). Later
Rabbis called the Law the most precious of possessions,
and compared its virtues to those of water, wine,
honey, milk and oil.[1]

In the other type there was a preponderating sense
of indebtedness to God for His gracious benefits.
The heavenly King was above all the benefactor—
'as the eyes of servants look unto the hand of their
master . . . so our eyes look unto the Lord our God, until
he have mercy upon us' (Ps. cxxiii. 2). There was
also an anticipation of the evangelical conversion of
later times. There is the wail of the sinner smitten by
terrors of conscience—'I have eaten ashes like bread,
and mingled my drink with weeping because of thine
indignation' (cii. 9). There is the joy of him who
has found salvation—'he brought me up also out of
an horrible pit, out of the miry clay . . . And he hath
put a new song in my mouth, even praise unto our
God' (xl. 2, 3). And there is the petition of the
penitent backslider—'wash me, and I shall be whiter
than snow . . . renew a right spirit within me'
(li. 7, 10).[2]

2. Notable work was also done by authority in the
religious and moral training of the mass of the people.
It was sought to impress a divine stamp upon the
nation, and to cast its whole life, political, economic

---

[1] Weber, *Judische Theologie*, 1897, p. 22.
[2] *Vide* Strachan: Art. 'Conversion,' *Encyclopaedia of Religion and Ethics.*

and domestic, in the moulds of a service of Jahweh. Every male child was claimed for God by the rite of circumcision. The family was hallowed by Paschal rites at which the father acted as priest and instructor. On one day in seven citizens were required, in the name both of piety and of humanity, to observe a day of rest. There were other stated festivals at which the people paid homage to God, renewed their covenant with Him, and were blessed in His name. Their climax was the arresting and thrilling rite of sacrifice, and this was accompanied from early times by some religious and moral instruction, which was greatly developed under the influence of Ezra.[1] In the post-exilic age the synagogue was the focus of the spiritual life of local communities, and it supplied the model of the Christian form of service in which the central position has been given to the reading and exposition of the word of God.

The results of this training seemed to be small indeed when judged by the absolute standard of the prophets. Amos pictured the northern Kingdom as devastated by immorality and cruelty (ii. 6 ff.), and Isaiah said of Judah that 'from the sole of the foot even unto the head there is no soundness in it; but wounds, and bruises, and putrifying sores' (i. 6). But the situation appears in another light when judged by the relative standard of the historian. It is to the credit of the organised religion that it eventually suppressed polytheism and idolatry, instilled into the general mind the fear of God as the guardian of the moral order, and created homes which were nurseries

---

[1] Ewald, *Geschichte Israels*, 1864, iv. p. 189.

of piety and virtue, and which from generation to generation sent forth men and women who made known to the nation the beauty of sainthood.

Of the two forms of conversion which have been distinguished a certain fusion was effected in the Jewish religion. Its primary aim was to produce a God-centred man, but the moral law which was proclaimed as the will of God had also constraining power. It improved on the theocentric type of heathenism by giving a better knowledge of God, and on the nomocentric type by putting duty to God in the first place. But the means of conversion at its disposal were inadequate. Prophets and saints had their vision of God, but when images were forbidden as aids to a realising sense of the invisible Being it could be felt by the sense-bound creature that he was left groping in the dark. On the ethical side the Old Testament ideal cannot be ranked higher than an instalment of the divine law. Moreover the dynamic was in need of strengthening for there was no certainty of a future life, while something was wanting in the messengers as well as in the message, to draw and bind souls to God with cords of love. To later prophets it seemed that what was chiefly needed was the gift from the source of life of a new heart, or a breath of God that would make the dry bones live (Ezek. xxxvi. 26).

From this summary review it appears that in the higher life of the ancient world there was a widespread sense of the need of a gospel of regeneration, and that many attempts were made to supply the needed means. A welcome was therefore assured to a credible religion which should undertake to effect a renewal of the natural man approved by heart and conscience. And these conditions were uniquely fulfilled in the Christian scheme of conversion. The foundations of it were laid in the Old Testament economy, while it borrowed from the Hellenistic schools some terms and ideas which served its theology, and some forms that were profitable for the religious life. But greater far was its debt to the Power which, as St. Paul said, and as was evident in his own work as an apostle, does new things in the history of the race. Whatever the precise debt of Christianity to earlier religions it should at least be agreed that, in comparison with the earlier efforts at conversion, the Christian scheme had the character of the perfected spiritual technique. For it propounded the noblest conception of the spirit and the endeavour of the new man, illustrated it by an example that rose to the height of the ideal, and made an unrivalled provision for the accomplishment of the task.

CHAPTER II

IN THE MINISTRY OF JESUS

THERE has been much debate in the schools of Biblical Criticism as to the special interests of the writers who compiled and edited the matter contained in our canonical Gospels. They had at least the common purpose of making Jesus known as the Son of God, and as the Saviour who quickens sinners into newness of life. The latest spoke for all when it was said to be written, 'that ye may believe that Jesus is the Christ, the Son of God; and that believing ye may have life in his name' (John xx. 31). The difference is that they show a growing perception of what was involved in these beliefs. For the Synoptists the climax of faith in Jesus was the confession that He was the promised Messiah (Mark viii. 29), while the fourth Gospel called for the greater confession that in Him 'the Word became flesh, and we beheld his glory, glory as of the only begotten from the Father' (John i. 14). There is also an ascending scale of teaching as to the nature and the genesis of the new man. Mark represented the work of conversion as central in the ministry of Jesus when he recorded the saying that the preaching of the Gospel was the end to which he came forth (i. 38), and he gave examples of the winning of souls along with pregnant sayings by which they were accompanied. For the author of Matthew's Gospel this didactic material was all too meagre, and he provided much detailed instruction as to the character and conduct required of the children of the Kingdom. Luke took a peculiar interest in the care of Jesus for wandering sheep and afflicted souls, and he added illuminating narratives and parables for greater encouragement and guidance in the labours of the evangelist. The fourth Gospel impressed on its readers that a purpose of the incarnation was the making of a new humanity, for it put in the forefront of the history the discourse with Nicodemus, in which it was taught that a man must undergo a change that makes him differ as radically from his former self as spirit differs from flesh, while it was made explicit that this regeneration rests on a divine initiative and is wrought by the Holy Spirit through water and the word (John iii. 5 ff., vi. 63).

The prolonged and microscopic scrutiny of the Synoptic Gospels has resulted in a consensus of critical opinion as to their origin and inter-connection. The positions now generally accepted are that Mark's Gospel, while based on the primitive testimony, was written at earliest about A.D. 60; that one or two decades later most of it was incorporated in Matthew's Gospel along with the substance of a Jewish Christian document cited as Q, and kindred memorabilia; and that about the same time Luke combined what he deemed most important in Mark and Q with kindred matter collected in his travels.[1] It would thus appear

---

[1] Streeter, *The Four Gospels*. The distinctive thesis of this English classic is that there was a first edition of Luke's Gospel founded on Q and later collections, and that in a second edition he co-ordinated with this about one-half of the Marcan Gospel.

that for a generation after Christ the oral tradition of the Church was the only available source of information regarding the life and teaching of Jesus, and the question is raised as to how far its content was due to a growing knowledge of the historical facts, how far to the faith and the practical requirements of the early Church.

The latest school of New Testament criticism has sought fresh light from an intensive study of the literary forms of the Gospels, and has inferred that the traditions which they embody were largely shaped by the popular mind, and especially by the ecclesiastical mind which desired to possess an increasingly effective instrument for the propagation of the faith and the edification of the flock. Analogy gives ground for supposing that the principal Churches, among them those of Rome and Antioch, felt the need of an easily accessible account of the work of the Saviour, that a trusted teacher was invited to prepare or put forward a worthy version, and that this was checked and amended in detail by a representative committee. This procedure would induce ecclesiastical accretions, but they were subject to a crucial historical test if, as is granted by a leading form-critic, 'the most important elements of the tradition were fixed in the twenty years following the death of Christ, and that at a time when eye-witnesses were still alive.' [1] Not least may we have confidence in the objectivity of the Synoptic reports of the work done by Jesus in the vocation of 'the shepherd and overseer of souls.' They were certainly not wholly

---

[1] Dibelius, *Formgeschichte des Evangeliums*, p. 295.

attuned to the later practice, for while in the apostolic
age the call to repentance was enforced by proclaiming
Jesus as the Messiah, it was here emphasised that the
disciples were left to discover the truth in the light
of what they had themselves found in Him, and that
it was a secret which they were forbidden to reveal
to the multitude (Mark viii. 30; Matt. xvi. 20).
They also gave it to be understood that, in contrast
with apostolic practice, the baptism with water was
not then required as a condition of entrance into the
Kingdom. In particular, we can feel assured of the
authenticity of the teaching concerning the change
of heart and the new life which was put forth in the
name of Jesus, for most of it has an individual
prophetic hall-mark, as well as a unity and sublimity
of content, which may not be ascribed to the co-
operative labour of the religious community. The
oral tradition conserved a mass of authentic material,
and the service of the Synoptists was that they drew
on it with progressive insight and skill. Streeter compared the picture in Mark to the snapshots of a
photographer, in Matthew and Luke to a portrait
by Rembrandt. 'Without Mark we should miss the
exacter details of a scene or two. . . . Later on, two
great, though perhaps unconscious, artists, trained in
the movement begun by the Master and saturated by
His spirit, retell the tale, idealise—if you like—the
picture, but in so doing make us realise something
of the majesty and the tenderness which men knew
in Galilee.' [1] The Johannine Gospel is primarily an
interpretation of the mission of Jesus in the light of

1 *Op. cit.*, pp. 194 ff.

His resurrection and return to the Father, written in reliance on the Holy Spirit, and so is chiefly utilised in New Testament Theology as a source for apostolic doctrine.

We proceed to give a summary view, mainly on the basis of the Synoptists, of the teaching of Jesus about the condition of natural man, and the character of the new man, of the methods which He employed in the conversion and sanctification of souls and of the general results of His work in the days of His flesh.[1]

I

THE NATURAL MAN

Jesus thought of mankind as exceeding sinful. He could not indeed forget that man bears the image of the heavenly Father, and He found in some so much to praise that on occasion He distinguished them as the good from the bad. Yet He spoke of man as by nature an evil being even as God is by nature holy (Matt. vii. 11). His own perfect purity made Him sensitive to the presence of sin in all its forms and under all disguises, and like the explorer of a dark continent He extended our vision of the range and the powers of the realm of evil.

His soul was stirred within Him by the thought of

---

[1] The teaching of Jesus according to the oldest sources is a capital theme of the modern Lives of Christ, and of the numerous works on N.T. Theology, which are among the most valuable of the latter-day contributions to the theological library. It is also the subject of many monographs that have had a wide influence on the Protestant pulpit, among which may be mentioned Wendt, *Die Lehre Jesu* ; A. B. Bruce, *The Kingdom of God* ; and T. W. Manson, *The Teaching of Jesus.*

heinous actual sins: the crimes, headed by murder, and the vices, headed by fornication and drunkenness, that fill the earth with violence and fraud, suffering and shame (Mark vii. 21 ff.). Among the worst of the sins of commission was named the corruption of 'the little ones,' and it was said of the culprit that 'it were better for him if a great millstone were hanged about his neck, and he were cast into the sea' (ix. 42). Sins of omission were judged no less sternly, for to have been deaf to the cries of human misery was given as reason enough for the final sentence—'depart from me, ye cursed' (Matt. xxv. 41 ff.). He saw a world of iniquity in the sins of the tongue—ranging from blasphemy against the Holy Ghost to the unconsidered offence of the idle word—and it was said that by our words we shall be justified or condemned (xii. 31 ff.). Very heinous also in His sight were the worst of the sins of thought, in which malicious feelings and impure imaginations are cherished with the intention of translating them into act at the convenient season—and it was said that he who is angry with his brother is akin to the murderer, and he who looks on a woman to lust after her was joined in condemnation with the adulterer (Matt. v. 22 ff.). To these was added the guilt of the dispositions which Theology has termed habitual sins. There was indeed no pronouncement on the question as to whether the natural bias to evil makes us guilty beings from the cradle, but at least the human heart was pictured as a well-spring of evil thoughts and desires which make for sin, and which being indulged by all give rise to sinful habitudes of the soul. Of these habitudes were specially mentioned covetousness, envy, pride and foolishness (Mark vii. 22), and the man of whose character they come to form the staple was likened to 'the corrupt tree that bringeth forth evil fruit' (Matt. vii. 17). And it may be said that they were summed up as selfishness, for this was identified as the badge of the natural man in the challenging words—'If any man would come after me, let him deny himself, and take up his cross, and follow me' (Mark viii. 34).

In truth, the charge against man as man was that he is essentially a self-centred being. Doubtless Jesus saw much in human conduct which has its spring in self-effacing love or a constraining sense of duty— kindness among neighbours, beneficence and fidelity in the relations of masters and servants, and much self-sacrificing service in the sphere of the family. But the urgent duty of the Good Physician was to fix attention on the prevailing spiritual malady, of which the most glaring forms are the self-indulgence that revels in the pleasures of sense, the ambition that schemes and strikes for place and power, the vanity that feeds on the praise of men, and above all the cupidity which seeks riches both because of its own glittering spell and for the pleasure, the power and the honour which it brings in its train. And it is the conception of self-seeking as the worst of sins, because the root of all evil that gives the key to the seemingly merciless indictment of the wealthy and the religious classes of His time.

The condemnation of the rich is reported in un- qualified terms—'Woe unto you that are rich! for ye have received your consolation. Woe unto you, ye that are full now! for ye shall hunger' (Luke vi. 24). To the same effect is the story of a certain man of whom nothing worse is recorded than that he was clothed in purple and fine linen, and fared sumptuously every day, yet who at death passed to the torments of Hades (xvi. 19 ff.). The rich men of Palestine in our Lord's day rendered no small economic services to the small and overcrowded country, and they were loyal to the religion of their fathers, but it was their class that provided the extreme examples of the self-centred life. Here were to be found the sensuality for which the value of life is that it is the opportunity to eat, drink and be merry (Luke xii. 19), an ambition like that of the great ones who lorded it over the Gentiles (Matt. xx. 25), and above all, a covetousness which was a heartfelt worship of Mammon. Moreover the promises of the Gospel made little appeal to the class which already possessed an attractive salvation in its large share of the goods of this world, and so it was said that 'it is easier for a camel to go through a needle's eye, than for a rich man to enter into the kingdom of God' (Mark x. 25).

In striking contrast to this judgment is the beautitude—'Blessed are ye poor: for yours is the kingdom of God. Blessed are ye that hunger now: for ye shall be filled' (Luke vi. 20-21). Assuredly it was not meant that poverty is of itself a passport to the Kingdom, and lest any should so think, Matthew reproduced a modified version—'Blessed are the poor in spirit. Blessed are they that hunger and thirst after righteousness' (Matt. v. 3, 6). The tribute to the poor meant in the original saying that in many ways they exemplified the spirit of self-sacrifice. They were humble, their lives were largely cast in the mould of useful while ill-requited toil, they were kind to one another, and they could be open-handed as the widow who cast into the temple-treasury 'the two mites which were all that she had, even all her living' (Mark xii. 41 ff.). Above all, they were disposed, with their experience of the distresses of the human lot, to welcome the great salvation, as shown by the fact that it was from among them that the main body of the disciples was gathered.

The so-called religious class was denounced in startling terms. The Pharisees, who were mostly laymen, had much to their credit : they ministered as teachers and preachers, they fostered sacred learning, they had signal success in getting a religious ideal accepted for public and private life, they upheld the cause of spiritual independence in conflict with kings and governors, and they were the backbone of the great missionary enterprise which spread the knowledge and worship of the true God in the surrounding heathen world. And without doubt there were not a few members of the sect besides Nicodemus and Saul of Tarsus who made it their chief business to know and to do the will of God. But the typical Pharisee was condemned as a self-worshipper, in that he courted popularity, coveted titles, claimed the chief places at feasts and in the synagogues, and glorified himself even when seeming to glorify God (Matt. vi. 2 ff., xxiii. 1 ff. ; Luke xviii. 11 ff.). The scribes were charged with devouring widows' houses (Mark xii. 40), though it appears that they had a defence in the plea that the spoil was devoted to the support of sacred learning and other good causes.

Those who were called sinners were a very mixed company. They were mainly the poor under another name, being branded as sinners because their occupations made it impossible to comply with the minute regulations of the ceremonial law. The class also included criminals, profligates and tax-gatherers. And it was a hard saying when it was said to the chief priests and elders, 'the publicans and the harlots go into the kingdom of God before you' (Matt. xxi. 31). But it meant no more than that in their shameful plight a strong appeal was made to them by the gospel of the forgiveness of sins with the prospect of a fresh start. And though it does not appear that any converts from this group were made apostles, there was at least a genuine succession that was made memorable by the pictures of the weeping Magdalene and the penitent thief.

Selfishness was primarily condemned by Jesus as a sin of impiety. It is a true idolatry, since it renders to a creature the honour and obedience due to the Creator, and as there is no room in the heart for two religions, the worship offered to God by the servant of self tends to become a hypocritical form (Matt. vi. 24). It also involves rebellion against God, even as the prodigal son threw off the parental yoke when he pleased himself by riotous living (Luke xv. 18), and the husbandmen who coveted the vineyard for themselves conspired against their master (Matt. xxi. 33 ff.). Selfishness was also exposed as the root of the sins of man against man. Much has been said

in modern times of the benefits accruing to society
when each does all that the law allows for his own
aggrandisement, but so far as this is true it can be
ascribed to the Providence which overrules evil for
good; and it has become ever clearer that the
contribution made by self-seeking to the well-being
of nations needs to be largely supplemented by
individuals and societies animated by the altruistic
spirit, and by governments that magnify their
ethical mission and claim a large share in the works
of beneficence and mercy.

II

THE NEW PATTERN

The marks of the new man are that he is knit to
God by filial devotion, to his fellow-creatures by
brotherly love, and that he accepts for himself the
obligation, which is likewise the privilege, of being in
the world as the servant of God and man.

Jesus spoke of the distinctive spirit of the new
creature as childlikeness—'Except ye turn, and become as little children, ye shall in no wise enter into
the kingdom of heaven' (Matt. xviii. 3). This meant
not merely that the disciple makes a new beginning,
but also that he recovers a childlike disposition, as
was made explicit in the saying that 'of such is the
kingdom of heaven' (xix. 14). The child was proposed as an example of humility because of his
constant sense of dependence on others, and he also
exemplifies the right attitude to God by his faith in

parental love and care, and his acceptance of parental
authority. It may in fact be said that the unspoken
parable underlying our Lord's teaching concerning
the Kingdom of God is that it is like unto a holy
family in which the children are bound to the parents
and also to one another by the cords of love and duty.

The new man of the Christian order, as in the Old
Testament school of piety, was primarily a man of
God. Jesus found the sum of piety in the ancient law—
'thou shalt love the Lord thy God with all thy heart,
and with all thy soul, and with all thy mind, and
with all thy strength' (Mark xii. 30; Deut. vi. 5).
And it was now added that the God of Moses and the
prophets was the heavenly Father whom the Son knew
and revealed to others (Matt. xi. 27). The emotional
side may not be overstressed, but at least the name
of Father bespoke filial affection toward God, and
the child was pictured as holding constant and
intimate communion with Him in prayer. Love of
God presupposes trust in His will and power to bless,
and the disciple was bidden to trust Him for the
great things of salvation—the forgiveness of sins,
succour in temptation (Matt. vi. 12, 13), the gift of
the Holy Spirit (Luke xi. 13) and the heavenly
inheritance (xii. 32), and also for a providential care
that extends to the urgent needs of the bodily life
(Matt. vi. 30 ff.). On the other hand, love of God
dictates as the fit beginning of prayer: 'Hallowed be
thy name. Thy kingdom come. Thy will be done,
as in heaven, so on earth' (Matt. vi. 9). And
it was obedience that was made the criterion at the
judgment—'Not every one that saith unto me, Lord,

Lord, shall enter into the kingdom of heaven; but
he that doeth the will of my Father which is in
heaven' (vii. 21). It was also shown by word and
deed that resignation to the will of God is a vital
form of filial obedience, and that in the hour when
His face is hidden and His arm seems to be shortened
the prayer of prayers is 'not what I will, but what
thou wilt' (Mark xiv. 36).

The mark of the new man in his relations with
others is that he takes to heart, and with a deeper
understanding, the old commandment, 'thou shalt
love thy neighbour as thyself' (Mark xii. 31; Lev.
xix. 18). And he was given to see a neighbour in
every one whom he found in distress, whether of
body or of soul, and whom it was in his power to
help (Luke x. 29 ff.). At the same time it was made
clear that the obligation to service has its special
objects and its diverse degrees. Jesus said that He
'was not sent but unto the lost sheep of the house of
Israel' (Matt. xv. 24). That it might be remembered
that the spiritual ties of the Kingdom of God are more
binding than the natural ties of home and kindred,
it was even said: 'If any man cometh unto me, and
hateth not his own father and mother, and wife, and
children, and brothers and sisters . . . he cannot be my
disciple' (Luke xiv. 26). The Johannine Gospel gives
it as the rule of the Christian society that the members
should love one another as Jesus had loved them
(xv. 12), and the degrees of intimacy were illustrated
by the privileges of the chosen three and the distinction of 'the disciple whom Jesus loved.' The
services to be rendered to those outside the Christian

family-circle were of many kinds. All were to have some share in ministering to the world of sin and suffering. A few were called to follow Jesus literally in the work of apostles and evangelists (Matt. x. 1 ff.; Luke x. 1 ff.). The many who continued in their callings were at least to be like unto the lamp 'that is put on the stand, and shineth unto all that are in the house' (Matt. v. 15). The minimum required of the ordinary disciple was that he should be in the world as a Good Samaritan. And the list of the works of mercy was engraven on his memory in words bound up with a haunting vision of the last judgment: 'I was an hungred, and ye gave me meat: I was thirsty, and ye gave me drink: I was a stranger, and ye took me in: naked, and ye clothed me: I was sick, and ye visited me: I was in prison, and ye came unto me' (Matt. xxv. 34 ff.).

The crowning grace of the new man in Christ Jesus is that he does good to those from whom he receives evil. He loves his enemies and prays for them that persecute him (Matt. v. 43), suffers wrong un-resistingly—even turns the other cheek to the smiter (v. 39), and forgives injuries unto seventy times seven (xviii. 21). Doubtless it was taken for granted that in concrete cases other considerations would be duly weighed, as that there is a duty of helping to protect society against fraud and violence, and also a duty to the evil-doer of helping to check him in a downward course. In a passage which seems to reflect the matured practice of the later Church it was enjoined that the injured member should first speak to his brother alone, that if this was declined he should propose a consultation with friends, that it might next be referred to the Church, and only in the last resort was the law to take its course as with a Gentile and a publican (Matt. xviii. 15 ff.).

With so much claimed in the service of God and man, self was greatly curbed and humbled. But there was no word of the asceticism that practises self-mortification for its own sake (Mark ii. 16). It was taken for granted that there is a care for self which is as laudable as it is necessary, for in the commandment self-love was accepted as the standard of brotherly love. Moreover love of God cannot become the master-principle without inspiring respect for one's own self as bearing the image of God, and embodying a unique thought of the Creator. It also inspires a sense of duty to one's own self, to the end that it may shine with more of the beauty of the divine original, and that the God-given talents may be used in furtherance of the special work that is given to each to do in the world. The call to man for self-renunciation thus became a promise of self-realisation, as has been found in the paradox—'whosoever would save his life shall lose it; and whosoever shall lose his life for my sake and the gospel's shall save it' (Mark viii. 35).

The new man as purposed by Jesus was thus radiant with piety and sympathy, at peace amid the storms of life and ennobled by a strain of heroism. The defect has been held to be that his mind was essentially other-worldly, whereby he was alienated and detached from the tasks of civilisation and culture that have been imposed on mankind by the conditions of existence on our planet. The criticism has support from the eschatological school of New Testament scholarship which finds that the teaching of Jesus was completely dominated by the conviction of the imminent destruction of the world; and that His Laws were therefore only applicable to those living in a disintegrated and vanishing order of things.[1] But there was also a strain of teaching, represented by the parables of the mustard-seed and the leaven, which implied that for a season the disciples would live under the conditions of the existing world-order (Matt. xiii. 31 ff.). And it does not appear that His principles are less applicable to a generation which believes that the race has a long career before it than to one which believed that an overwhelming cataclysm was impending. It does not make much difference to the individual which expectation is correct, as he spends his days under a sentence of death which may be carried out at any moment, and has to reckon with the menace of apocalyptic happenings in another world than is entered by the gate of death. When it became clear that God has purposed a prolonged probation and leavening of the race, it was realised that the teaching of Jesus not only permits but encourages the general body of His disciples to make full use of their God-given talents in the secular spheres of necessary and honourable toil. The commandment to love our neighbour as ourselves was also seen to have very important social bearings, since for most the chief way of obeying it is by diligent and faithful service in a useful calling, and in the life of the

[1] J. Weiss, *Die Predigt Jesu*, 1900, p. 138.

home. Moreover, when the central place in heart and mind is given to God, it is far from entailing the loss of intellectual and aesthetic interests; rather may it be that a science has for a believer the additional attraction that in it he studies his Father's works and thinks His thoughts after Him, while in devoting his powers to literature or the Fine Arts he can feel himself a fellow-worker with the Creator who unfolded on earth the most enthralling of dramas, and enriched the environment with the splendours of the firmament, the music of birds and the beauty of flowers.

III

The Call to the Unconverted

The work of Jesus in the remaking of souls began with a call of sinners to repentance. At this point we consider the means of persuasion that He used, and the nature of the experience that was accepted as evidence of the required change of heart.

1. Not least among the means of persuasion was the personality of the prophet of whom it was said that 'he taught them as having authority,' and that 'never man so spake' (Mark i. 22; John vii. 46). Faith in the teacher was increased by the fame of His mighty works, and men reasoned as is reported of Nicodemus—'we know that thou art a teacher come from God: for no man can do those signs that thou doest, except God be with him' (John iii. 2). It was therefore sought to undermine His authority by showing that His teaching and practice were

contrary to the divine laws given by Moses (Mark ii. 23 ff., x. 3 ff.), and to discount the miracles of healing as wrought with the help of the prince of the devils (iii. 22).

The call to a change of heart was enforced by two lines of argument. What was primarily impressed upon the sinner was that it was a matter of life and death that he should repent and turn to God. The promise was that he would thus enjoy the favour and friendship of the Father on earth, and that great would be his reward in heaven (Matt. v. 3 ff., vi. 33). It was also sought to draw men to the Kingdom by the promise that those who took His yoke upon them would have rest of soul (Matt. xi. 28). The warning was that by continuing in his evil ways he makes an enemy of his Maker, and that the final portion of the impenitent is a hell whose terrors were summed up as 'the eternal fire' or as 'the outer darkness' where there shall be 'weeping and gnashing of teeth' (Matt. xviii. 8, viii. 12).

It has been an offence to some philosophical minds that the method used to lead sinners to repentance was to stir them by the fear of punishment and the hope of rewards. But if there be a future life which is a state of retribution—and the doctrine is a vital part of the Christian revelation—it may well be deemed an urgent duty as well as a kindness to make it known and persuade sinners to believe it. And as it was the natural man whom the evangelist addressed, he was most likely to be moved by the argument that it is the height of folly to persevere in the rebellious course, and the height of wisdom to make a new beginning in the service of a reconciled God. It may in fact be ascribed to the wisdom of Him who knew what is in man that He began by enlisting the self in discrediting selfishness, and thus induced the sinner to enter on a new life in which he goes on to discover that there is a unique joy in unselfish service, and that the self-denying virtues are well worth possessing for their own sake. It should also be observed by the critic that Jesus made no small use of arguments which appeal to the altruistic side of human nature. One was that as we owe to God our existence, and have also received from Him great and undeserved mercies, the fitting response is that we should trust and obey Him, and especially that we should imitate the clemency and the loving-kindness of the heavenly Father (Matt. v. 48). Again, one of the redeeming features of the natural man is a sense of justice, with its demand to render to all their due, and it may be said that Jesus sought an auxiliary in this quarter when He bade men do to others as they would that they should do to them (Matt. vii. 12). And he could reckon on sympathy with the sufferings of our fellow-creatures, another of the better natural qualities, to help to win acceptance for the model of the Good Samaritan.

2. The essence of conversion was sometimes described as repentance. In the full sense of the term this meant a complete change of heart, with a corresponding change of life, but in the first instance Jesus was satisfied with an instalment that involved a decided breach with the old life, and gave promise that the good work would be carried to completion. It was now one, now another, moment of the change

of heart that was accepted as the one thing needful. Usually it was repentance in the sense of contrition for a sin-stained past—as expressed in the tears of the woman in the city that was a sinner, the confession of the publican in the temple, and the remorse of the dying malefactor. Faith was also accepted as sufficient, and it was said, 'thy faith hath saved thee' (Luke vii. 50). By this was meant a great trust which had as its object God and His promises, and especially Himself as the Saviour sent from God. Jesus also spoke of love for Himself as the condition of salvation, for it was said of the woman in the city that her sins were forgiven because she loved much (Luke vii. 47), and the devotion of the Mary who sat at His feet was declared to be the good part, which should not be taken away from her (x. 42). A signal act of self-denial was also treated as good evidence of a conversion—Zacchaeus was called a son of Abraham because he gave half his goods to feed the poor (Luke xix. 8), and it seems that the young ruler would have been within the Kingdom and not only near to it had he passed what was for him the final test of self-renunciation (Mark x. 21). On the other hand, these experiences were so vitally connected that one could be said to vouch for the presence or the coming of the others. And each form of the response contributed materially to the dissolution of the old man. Contrition meant that his pride was humbled; faith, that his self-sufficiency gave place to childlike dependence on divine grace; and a heart-felt love of God or of His Christ, that self-seeking was displaced as the governing principle of

D

the life. And manifestly the natural centre of gravity was radically changed when a man resolved to follow Jesus wherever He went, though knowing that the Son of Man had not where to lay His head.

IV

The Training of the Converts

The training was of two kinds suited to the looser and the stricter forms of discipleship.

The great majority abode in their homes and callings. When Jesus was in their neighbourhood they followed Him from place to place that they might hear more of His gracious words, and on occasion they sat down with Him in companies at a meal that foreshadowed the love-feast of a later age. When He departed from them there were doubtless gatherings of disciples in Capernaum and other centres at which they received news of His mission, and also called to remembrance the things they had themselves seen and heard. There would also be suppers of the character of which we have a glimpse in Bethany (Mark xiv. 3 ff.).

Much more intensive was the training of the chosen band who accompanied the Master on His journeys. They lived in the atmosphere of prayer, and there is some record of thanksgivings and intercessions which were offered by Jesus in presence of the disciples (Matt. xi. 25; John xvii. 1 ff.). They were bidden to be much in prayer to the Father which seeth in secret (Matt. vi. 6)—even as He himself was wont to go into a mountain apart, and in Gethsemane sought

to be alone with God (Matt. xiv. 23, xxvi. 36).
'All things,' He said, 'whatsoever ye shall ask in
prayer, believing, ye shall receive' (Matt. xxi. 22),
and they were assured importunity surely prevails
with God in the end (Luke xviii. 1 ff.).   There was
constant instruction, in which hard sayings were
explained and the spirit of the new law was illustrated
and enforced, with the crowning privilege that they
found in the Teacher the perfect example of the graces
that were enjoined.   They were also under a salutary
discipline as the Master gave them to see themselves
as God saw them, while flagrant breaches of the laws
of the Kingdom called forth the indignation of the
fraternity (Mark x. 41).   The growth of the Christlike character was also furthered by the prescription
of Christlike tasks. Most important in this kind
was the sending forth of the twelve and the seventy
to extend the work of the Saviour, and to carry it on
by His methods and in the spirit of the Sermon on
the Mount (Matt. x. 5 ff.; Luke x. 1 ff.).   Provision
had to be made for the temporal wants of the inner
circle, and we hear of rich men who gave hospitality,
and of certain women, Mary called Magdalene,
Joanna the wife of Chuza, Herod's steward, and
Susanna, and many others, 'which ministered unto
them of their substance' (Luke viii. 2).

V

THE RESULTS

The immediate fruits of the ministry of Jesus were
small in respect both of the number and the quality

of the converts. To the people as a whole He applied
the words of the prophet: 'their heart is waxed gross,
and their ears are dull of hearing, and their eyes they
have closed' (Matt. xiii. 15). At one time the
Galileans would have made Him a king, but the
enthusiasm died down when they learned that He
was not a political Saviour, and that while the
worldly hopes were unfounded the stern demands
remained. When in Jerusalem He was brought to
the judgment-seat of Pilate, the demand of the
multitude was, 'Crucify him' (Mark xv. 13). In
the incidents related of the best of the disciples the
point often is that they fell far short of the standard
of the new man both in goodness and intelligence.
The sons of Zebedee showed themselves proud and
vindictive (Mark x. 35; Luke ix. 54), and when
Peter was in danger of sharing the fate of the Master
he denied with curses that he so much as knew Him
(Mark xiv. 71). When the Shepherd was slain and
the sheep scattered, it seemed that the Galilean mission
had ended in tragic failure. Despite the passing cry,
'Why hast thou forsaken me?' (Mark xv. 34), Jesus
knew that the gates of Hades would not prevail
(Matt. xvi. 18), and that in the hour of the power
of darkness His thought of the disciples was that
voiced in the words, 'My father hath given them to
me, and no one is able to snatch them out of the
Father's hand' (John x. 29). But had the last chapter
of His earthly life been the story of the crucifixion,
He would probably only have been remembered,
if indeed His name had not been blotted out, as the
gentle Rabbi who magnified the goodness of the

Almighty, and sought to infuse into Hebrew piety more of the spirit of loving-kindness. What happened was that the message was so enriched and strengthened by new things wrought by God that the works of the disciples were greater than those of their Lord (John xiv. 12).

Chapter III

IN THE PRIMITIVE CHURCH

THE apostolic mission began by making converts among the Jews of Palestine and the Diaspora, it had greater results when it turned to the Gentiles, and within three centuries Christianity had become the official religion of the Roman Empire. Much has been written to explain the paradox of its popularity, and Gibbon's list of five causes has been increased to over twenty by later historians.[1] The lowest social class was attracted to the Church as an institution which gave them dignity and laboured to relieve their distresses. Some of the intellectual class found in its doctrines a popular version of ethical theism, and later emperors patronised it as a useful ally in civil war and a promising bulwark of law and morality. But the primary cause was that Christianity was superior as a religion to its rivals, and that many to whom the Gospel was preached were able to appreciate its pre-eminence. It made the strongest appeal to man as a spiritual being by offering a great salvation which in wide circles was felt to be sorely needed, which depended on the one true God and a Saviour with divine credentials, and with whose gracious conditions it seemed easy to comply. It was also

[1] *Decline and Fall of the Roman Empire*, chap. xv. Harnack, *Die Mission und Ausbreitung des Christentums*, 1902, pp. 357 ff.

54

impressively commended, as Gibbon observed, by the fact that it produced a type of piety in which austerity and heroism were blended with loving-kindness. Above all, there was a sense of the working of a supernatural power which crowned the missionary labours with an abundant harvest (Acts ii. 47; 1 Cor. i. 6).

Our concern is with the new humanity which in the primitive period could be reckoned the staple of the Christian society, and with the message and the methods which produced the extraordinary spiritual results.

I

THE WORK OF CONVERSION

The apostolic age began with conversions on a large scale. When Peter preached to the multitude at Pentecost three thousand souls received his word and were baptized (Acts ii. 41). Soon afterwards the number of those in Jerusalem obedient to the faith had risen to five thousand, among whom was 'a great company of the priests' (iv. 4, vi. 7). In the mission to the Gentiles there were disappointments, but the usual experience was that the Gospel came unto them 'in power and in the Holy Ghost and in much assurance' (1 Thess. i. 5), and the foundations were laid of growing and enduring Churches. From the beginning of the second century it was claimed that a new race had sprung up which was to be ranked as a third with Jews and Gentiles, and destined to absorb them.[1]

---

[1] *Epistle to Diognetus*, 1, 5. *Apology of Aristides*, 2.

1. The essential content of the experience was faith in Christ as the Saviour, and a repentance which had the depth of a change of heart. These were vitally connected, and either of them could be emphasised as the condition of acceptance with God, and as the beginning of the new life. When the awakened multitude asked of Peter, 'What shall we do?' the reply was, 'Repent ye, and be baptized . . . in the name of Jesus Christ unto the remission of your sins' (Acts ii. 37-38). When the Philippian jailor asked of Paul and Silas, 'What must I do to be saved?' the reply was, 'Believe on the Lord Jesus, and thou shalt be saved, thou and thy house' (xvi. 31). The conversion of Saul of Tarsus had exceptional features, but it illustrated the normal sequence of events in that he was constrained to believe in the risen Lord, repented in fasting and prayer of his unbelief and rebellion, was baptized and received into the Christian society, and went his way rejoicing in the gracious forgiveness of his sins, and purposing to bring forth fruits meet for repentance (ix. 1 ff.). In the Epistles conversion was spoken of as a resurrection from the dead (Rom. vi. 4), a creative act (2 Cor. v. 17) and a second birth (1 Pet. i. 23); and it is evident that in these terms, astounding though they were, readers and hearers recognised a familiar experience.

2. The capital instrument in this work was the preaching of the Gospel. 'It was God's good pleasure,' said Paul, 'through the foolishness of the preaching, to save them that believe' (1 Cor. i. 21). 'The word of God,' said the writer to the Hebrews, 'is living, and active, and sharper than any two-edged sword'

(iv. 12). In particular, it was emphasised that through the word of God they were begotten again (1 Pet. i. 23) or brought forth to be 'a kind of first-fruits of his creatures' (Jas. i. 18).

The core of the missionary message was the witness to Christ as Saviour and Lord. The preacher to the Jews assumed a knowledge of the true God whose will was revealed in the Law and the Prophets, and he hastened to tell of great things wrought by God in the latter days. The sum of it was that Jesus of Nazareth whom they had rejected and crucified was the Son of God, that He had been raised from the grave, that He now reigned in glory to bless them, that He would return to judge the world, and that there was 'no other name under heaven, that is given among men, wherein we must be saved' (Acts ii. 22 ff., iv. 8 ff.). In the approach to the Gentiles the twofold call was 'to turn unto God from idols,' and 'to wait for his Son from heaven, whom God raised from the dead' (1 Thess. i. 10). It has been thought that Paul blamed himself for discoursing philosophy to the men of Athens instead of preaching the Gospel, but it was necessary to begin with a witness to the true God whom they ignorantly wor-shipped, and before the interruption he had come to speak of the Man whom God had ordained as Saviour, of His resurrection from the dead, and of His return to judge the world in righteousness (Acts xvii. 31). Of the Gentiles also faith in the Messiah was required as the condition of salvation, but with a growing perception that this title did not reveal the full glory of the Son of God. It was therefore made explicit in the later Pauline Epistles, as in Hebrews and the fourth Gospel, that the Christ was not a man who had been raised to the sphere of Godhead, but the unique Son who from the beginning existed in the form of God, through whom the works of creation and providence were wrought, and who for the work of redemption took 'the form of a servant, being made in the likeness of men' (Phil. ii. 7; Col. i. 16; Heb. i. 1 ff.; John i. 1 ff.).

It was a great venture of faith that was asked of the Jews when they were bidden to believe that Jesus of Nazareth, the teacher and healer who had been put to death as a malefactor and seemingly by the just judgment of God, had been delivered from the grave, and raised or restored to the height of divine dignity and power. Belief was made humanly possible by the fact that it was the passionate conviction of disciples who hazarded their lives in proclaiming it, and who also gave strong reasons for their faith. That Jesus rose from the dead was vouched for by the apostles and many others who claimed to have seen and held converse with Him after the crucifixion. That He now lived and reigned in the heavenly sphere was declared to be proved by the miraculous powers bestowed on the servants who continued His saving work, and also by the enrichment of the souls of believers with the gifts of the Holy Spirit (Acts ii. 33). The second compelling proof was that the events of His earthly mission had been divinely protected, and in particular that God had 'foreshewed by the mouths of all the prophets, that his Christ should suffer' (Acts iii. 18).

To the Gentiles reasons were given for believing in
the God of Abraham and the prophets. That there
is a God was common ground with the missionary
and the typical heathen audience. What God is in
His sovereign perfections, Paul taught, was revealed
in the works of creation—'the invisible things are
clearly seen, being perceived through the things that
are made, even his everlasting power and divinity.'
They had indeed 'exchanged the truth for a lie, and
worshipped and served the creature rather than the
Creator,' but this was because they became 'vain in
their reasonings,' and the evidence and punishment
of their departure from the truth was that wickedness had come in like a flood (Rom. i. 16 ff.). In
His mercy God had now 'shined out of darkness to
give the light of the knowledge of his glory in the
face of Jesus Christ' (2 Cor. iv. 6). In proof of the
divine mission of Christ the main stress was laid, as
among the Jews, on the attested miracle of the resurrection of Christ and the fulfilment in Him of Old
Testament prophecies. The idea of a Jewish Messiah
would rather be repugnant to other peoples, but the
picture of the Saviour bespoke the sympathy of those
who worshipped children of Zeus as signal benefactors
of mankind, and especially of votaries of the mystery-
cults. The decision was not difficult when the choice
lay between a reputed member of the Olympian
family or an Egyptian goddess, and the only-begotten
Son of the infinite God—whom eyes had seen and
hands had touched (1 John i. 1). Paul found that
the doctrine of the crucified Saviour was deemed
foolishness among Greeks, even as to the Jews it was

a stumbling-block (1 Cor. i. 23), but there was a
growing revelation of the magnetism of the Cross as
foretold in the Johannine saying of the Lord—'I, if
I be lifted up from the earth, will draw all men unto
myself' (John xii. 32).

The witness to the crucified and risen Christ greatly
strengthened the call to repentance. The Jews believed in a righteous God who punishes iniquity, they
had been stirred by the Baptist's announcement of
an approaching judgment, and it was now laid to
their charge that they had 'killed the Prince of life'
whom God had sent to save them from their sins
(Acts iii. 15). Moreover, they were given to fear that
it was the Christ whose blood was upon them and
their children by whom they would be judged at the
last day. In the case of the Gentiles the indictment
would rather be on the lines of the Epistle to the
Romans, in which it was shown that they also had
grievously sinned against the light vouchsafed to
them, and so were deserving of condemnation and
death (Rom. i. 18 ff.). There was in truth ground
enough for condemnation in the folly of heathen
superstitions, and in the vices and crimes that cried
to heaven from the cities of the Graeco-Roman
world.

In the apostolic preaching, as in the ministry of
Jesus, it was thus primarily sought to move sinners
to repentance by the dynamic of a great fear and a
great hope. The typical missionary addresses in Acts
issued in the call to repent and believe as the only
way of escaping the wrath to come, and of entering
into the Kingdom of heaven. The main themes of

the Apocalypse were the doom of the world lying in wickedness, and the security and the glories of the heavenly Jerusalem. Believing Jews were given to think of Christianity as, above all, the religion of hope, with the vision of 'an inheritance incorruptible, and undefiled, and that fadeth not away, reserved in heaven' (1 Pet. i. 4). Paul also made much use of the terrors of the Lord to persuade men (2 Cor. v. 11). In the Epistle to the Romans the cardinal boon of the Gospel was set forth as a justification consisting in acceptance with God and remission of sins, which is followed in this life by an instalment of the privileges of the children of God, and in eternity by a heaven transcending all that eye has seen, and ear heard, and that has entered into the heart of man (1 Cor. ii. 9).

On the other hand, there was a signal reinforcement, as the result of the passion and the resurrection of Christ, of the altruistic arguments for a change of heart and newness of life. In the teaching of Jesus there was a call to goodness in imitation of the heavenly Father, and to the knowledge of His beneficence in the realm of nature was now added the revelation of self-sacrifice in the inner life of the Godhead, in that 'God so loved the world, that he gave his only begotten Son' (John iii. 16), and 'commendeth his own love toward us, in that, while we were yet sinners, Christ died for us' (Rom. v. 8). It was also proclaimed as the supreme privilege of the Gospel that it translates the believer into a realm of love in which 'the life is hid with Christ in God' (Col. iii. 3), and of which the description was given in the name of Christ—'if a man love me he will keep my word; and my Father will love him, and we will come unto him, and make our abode with him' (John xiv. 23). There was also a strengthened appeal to the divine strain in human nature which recognises the imperative of the moral law, and disposes us to think that the good chiefly to be desired for man is the power to be ever loyal to the ideal. Paul wrote on occasion as if the crowning blessing of the salvation purchased by Christ is the deliverance from the dominion of sin that has been made possible by the gracious deliverance from its guilt (Rom. vii. 24). The Epistle of James reveals a teacher for whom Christianity was, above all, the religion of the perfected law, providing the will and the power to obey it that spring from the word ingrafted into the soul (i. 21).

The efficacy of preaching in the work of conversion was increased by the practice of baptism. The ordinance was enjoined in the charge of the risen Lord to the apostles (Matt. xxviii. 19), and doubtless it rendered a unique service in the evangelistic mission. When a sinner was awakened and was halting between two opinions, this provision would bring matters to a head and impel to a decision, and many must have looked back to the hour when they were baptized as the turning-point in their spiritual history. So profound was the sense of the difference made by baptism that it was spoken of as 'the washing (or 'the laver') of regeneration' (Titus iii. 5), and in the latest Gospel, water was conjoined as an instrument with the Spirit in the discourse on the necessity of the new birth (John iii. 5). Normally, however, it merely attested and confirmed a conversion which had already taken place, since those only were received to baptism who had made a credible profession of faith in Christ and repentance unto life. What it added on the part of the subject was the act of obedience of which it was said: 'Every one who shall confess me before men, him will I also confess before my Father which is in heaven. But whosoever shall deny me before men, him will I also deny before my Father which is in heaven' (Matt. x. 32). What it added from the side of God could be termed regeneration, but as the conversion presupposed in baptism was nothing less than a second birth, the baptismal experience has naturally been distinguished from it in Theology as an increase of spiritual life and power falling within the sphere of sanctification.

II

THE SCHOOL OF SANCTIFICATION

There is a marked contrast between the ideal Church as represented by its divine programme and its élite, and the empirical Church in which the work of the Holy Spirit is much opposed and obscured by unsubdued forces of human nature. The New Testament writers, however, did not stress the distinction, as in the primitive period the marvel of the achievement eclipsed the shortcomings.

A prediction of John the Baptist was quoted as having been fulfilled in Christ—'I baptize you with water, but he that cometh after me shall baptize you

with the Holy Ghost and with fire' (Matt. iii. 11).
By this was commonly understood a physical state of
excitement and rapture, but it included many forms
of a holy passion which flamed in the soul of the
Church, even as the seer of Patmos saw in a vision
'seven lamps of fire burning before the throne' (Rev.
iv. 5). The list might run as follows: zeal for the
glory of God, adoration of Christ, jealousy for the
truth, the hunger and thirst after righteousness, the
desire of saving souls, love of the brethren and sympathy with suffering humanity. Each was illustrated
by the regenerated Saul of Tarsus, and if devotion
to Christ and missionary zeal were most in evidence,
there was also a constant purpose of subjecting the
old man to the yoke of Christ, and of attaining to
love those who despitefully used him and persecuted
him (Rom. xii. 19; Phil. iii. 12). The first apostles
grew up to the stature of the perfect man in Christ
Jesus. Peter atoned for the temporary apostasy by
fearless courage in the service of the risen Lord, and
the John who had been rebuked for the contrary
faults was remembered as one who by word and
example inculcated the graces of humility and
brotherly love. A Christian Church shone in the
darkness of the pagan world as a society whose
members were dedicated to a life of communion with
the all-holy God, of purity and uprightness, and of
the loving service of the afflicted and the destitute.
The Corinthian Church had its scandals, but the
general body was addressed as ' sanctified in Christ
Jesus' (1 Cor. i. 2). The sternest of censors witnessed
of the Church in Ephesus that 'it did bear for Christ's

sake, and had not grown weary,' and of the Church
in Thyatira that it was 'great in love and faith and
ministry and patience, and that its last works were
more than the first' (Rev. ii. 3, 19). Towards the
end of the first century Clement of Rome wrote to
the Church in Corinth: 'Who ever dwelt even for a
short time among you, and did not find your faith
to be as fruitful of virtue as it was firmly established?
Ye stretched forth your hands to God Almighty, beseeching Him to be merciful unto you, day and night
ye were anxious for the whole brotherhood, forgetful
of injuries between one another and ready to every
good work, the commandments and ordinances of the
Lord were written upon the table of your hearts.'[1]
Another of the same period claimed for Christians
these features of the new humanity: 'They pass their
days on earth but they are citizens of heaven, they
obey the prescribed laws, and at the same time
surpass the laws by their lives, they love all men and
are persecuted by all, they are poor yet make many
rich, they are reviled and bless, when punished
they rejoice as if quickened into life.'[2] There was
now on earth, it was said, a veritable temple of
God—'having received the forgiveness of sins, we
have become new creatures formed again from the
beginning, . . . He himself prophesying in us, He himself dwelling in us.'[3] There was at least so much truth
in the picture that the first apologists of the second
century made great use of the argument that a religion

---

[1] *First Epistle*, chaps. i. and ii. (condensed).
[2] *Epistle to Diognetus*, chap. v. (condensed).
[3] *Epistle of Barnabas*, chap. xvi.

E

whose products had so much of the divine must have God for its author.[1]

The proximate causes of this rich spiritual life were the radical character of the conversions, and the intensive training by which the Church built up its members in holiness and righteousness.

1. The primitive type of conversion made for a high degree of piety and virtue. The sense of unmerited mercy of God in Christ awoke in the pardoned a gratitude which impelled them no longer 'to live unto themselves, but unto him who for their sakes died and rose again' (2 Cor. v. 15). They called Christ Master and Lord, in baptism they had vowed Him allegiance, and it was felt to be an elementary duty to seek to obey His commandments and follow His example (John xiii. 15). They were even those who felt that it had become their second nature to do Christlike works, as their conversion meant nothing less than that they had died and Christ lived in them (Gal. ii. 20). They were incited to greater diligence by the hope that at the last 'each shall receive his own reward according to his own labour' (1 Cor. iii. 8), while they were warned that by heinous sins they would 'crucify the Son of God afresh' (Heb. vi. 6), and invite a judgment like that which struck down Ananias and Sapphira (Acts v. 1 ff.).

2. The Church addressed itself strenuously, with the aid of additional means of grace, to the work of perfecting the converts in the love of God and man.

(a) The primary aim, as prescribed by Jesus, was

[1] *Apology of Aristides.*

to ensure that God had the central place in the inner
life of the disciples, and that in Him they found their
strength and their stay. The example of communion
with God was set by the apostles, who 'continued
stedfastly in prayer, with the women, and Mary the
mother of Jesus, and with his brethren' (Acts i. 14).
They also met with Him in the temple at the daily
service of prayer and sacrifice, and on the Sabbath
in the worship of the synagogue. The distinctively
Christian worship began in private houses, at which
there was thanksgiving to God who had exalted the
Crucified 'to be a Prince and a Saviour,' and supplication that His servants, supported by 'signs and
wonders done through his name,' might 'speak the
word in all boldness' (iv. 23 ff.). When many were
added to the Church, the assemblies still continued
to be on the model of those at which Jesus supped
with His disciples and discoursed of the things of the
Kingdom of God. The course of the development of
the public worship is obscure, in particular the place
of the Lord's Supper in the context of the social
intercourse, but we at least know what was included
in the proceedings, and that all concurred to produce
a profound sense of the presence and power of the
living God. His voice was heard when, as in the
synagogue, passages were read from the Law and the
prophets, and to these was now added some instruction from the words spoken through His Son in the
latter days. That God was with them as the Holy
Ghost was specially felt when with the teaching and
the praises were mingled the rapt utterances of the
speakers with tongues, and the impassioned witness

and the revelations of those who prophesied (1 Cor. xiv. 26). The Lord's Supper strengthened the ties that knit the believers to the Son of God, and this in the several ways stressed in one or more of the accounts of the institution (1 Cor. xi. 23-26; Mark xiv. 22-25; Matt. xxvi. 26-29; Luke xxii. 14-20). It gave them to remember the death of Jesus when, because of His sufferings and their loss, sorrow could fill their hearts. The sorrow was turned into joy when they were reminded in treasured words that it was by His blood He sealed the new covenant which brought the remission of their sins, and when they looked forward to the renewal of the hallowed intimacy in the Father's Kingdom. They were recalled to the present to find the risen Lord in their midst, giving them of His broken body and shed blood for the nourishment of their souls unto eternal life. Doubtless there were those who thought that they did literally ' eat the flesh of the Son of Man and drink his blood,' but Paul insisted that the risen Lord has a spiritual body, and they were to be expressly corrected by the fourth Gospel, which, while using these terms, warns that 'it is the spirit that quickeneth; the flesh profiteth nothing' (John vi. 63).

(b) Much was also done to train the disciples to love their neighbours as themselves. In the religious services there was detailed instruction in the laws of Jesus, which would be enforced by the admonition that 'he that loveth not his brother whom he hath seen, cannot love God whom he hath not seen' (1 John iv. 20). And as practice does more than

precept for the building of character, the members
of the primitive Church had much exercise in the
service of others. The Christian society was modelled
as far as practicable on that of the family-circle. The
members associated on the footing of brothers and
sisters in Christ, of which a chief expression was the
love-feast at which the rich and poor, the learned
and unlearned, ate and drank at one table, and held
converse as joint possessors of the privileges of the
heavenly citizenship. The first Christians were encouraged to think that as brethren they should share
all earthly goods, and those were highly esteemed
who 'being possessors of lands or houses sold them,
and brought the prices and laid them at the apostles'
feet' (Acts iv. 34). But the historian emphasises that
it was never made compulsory, and the apostle did
not even suggest it to the Gentile Christians. The
binding principle, of which this was the most impressive illustration, was that to the utmost of his
power each should do good to those who were of the
household of faith (Gal. vi. 10). It was counted a
primary duty to minister to the needs of the destitute
and the afflicted members of the flock, and also to
welcome as kinsmen the passing strangers who had
been commended as brethren in the Lord (Rom. xii.
10; Heb. xiii. 2). Disputes between Christians were
to be settled in the spirit of brotherly love, and the
appeal to the legal tribunal was discountenanced
(1 Cor. vi. 7). Grave breaches of the laws of the
family, especially in the matter of purity, were matter
of ecclesiastical discipline, and flagrant and obdurate
transgressors were cast out (1 Cor. v. 1 ff.).

The wider brotherly love, whose object is man as man, was also fostered. It was recognised that the heathen had a claim to the offices of the Good Samaritan, though in secular relations with un-believers attention was mainly confined to the duties of 'taking thought for things honourable in the sight of all men,' living if possible 'at peace with all men,' and 'rendering to no man evil for evil' (Rom. xii. 17). In the outside world the most important form of service was the missionary enterprise enjoined by the risen Lord, which was led and guided by apostles and commissioned evangelists, promoted by travellers and traders in distant parts, and supported by the faith and the prayers of the mother-churches.

We have noted the immediate causes of the extra-ordinary access of power that was manifest in the life and labours of the primitive Church. In the field of conversion the chief factor was the enrichment and confirmation of the message by the witness to the resurrection of Christ and the significance of His passion. What is chiefly needed to move sinners to repentance is a vision of the holy and loving God, and they were now given to see Him imaged, not merely in the pale and broken reflection of human fatherhood, but in the splendour of the only-begotten Son who out of love to man became man and drank the cup of human suffering to the dregs, who now reigned in heaven as the mighty Saviour, and who would return to judge the world in righteousness. The spell of a lofty ideal felt by an élite of mankind was also strengthened, for the teaching of the Sermon on the Mount was now illustrated by the Master's own example of obedience unto death, and made more practicable by the assurance of the needed enduement of power. In the field of sanctification the new provision was the existence in the Church of a worship which fostered an intimate union with the living God, and of a fellowship which inspired brotherly love and engaged the brethren in manifold forms of Christlike service. It was, however, the divine causality on which the apostolic mind chiefly dwelt, when there was occasion to explain the extraordinary events and experiences. To God was given the glory as the author of the great salvation, and of the means of grace that equipped the Church for its saving mission. To the Holy Ghost, God manifest in the Church, was ascribed the office of making the means of grace effectual in the conversion of sinners and the sanctification of the faithful. It was also taught that there was something incalculable in the movements of the Spirit, even as 'the wind bloweth where it listeth, and thou knowest not whence it cometh, and whither it goeth' (John iii. 8). If without the Spirit the work of man was fruitless, its greatest gifts could also be imparted without the use of the ordinary means. Of the same message addressed by the same preacher to people of like sort it was observed that in one city it fell on deaf ears, and in another moved mind and will by the demonstration of the Spirit and of power. There was the same contrast between different periods, for later Fathers looked back to the apostolic age as the time of boundless liberality, while they were conscious of a growing parsimony that implied neglect and even threatened desertion by the Lord and Giver of life. Yet there were two laws by which it was believed that the operations of the Holy Ghost were bound. One was that Spirit was alienated and could be quenched as the result of unfaithfulness in the use of the gracious gifts (1 Thess. v. 19). Another was that the presence of the Spirit is assured in response to believing and importunate prayer (Luke xi. 13). And we know that the God with whom we have to do is faithful to His promises. Paul traced an inviolable sequence in the experience of those whom God had once decisively claimed as His own—'whom he foreknew, he also foreordained: and whom he foreordained, them he also called: and whom he called, them he also justified: and whom he justified, them he also glorified' (Rom. viii. 30). He agonized over the tragedy of the chosen people who seemed to have rejected themselves in rejecting the Messiah, but he trusted that 'when the fulness of the Gentiles is come in, all Israel shall be saved' (Rom. xi. 25). Still less could he doubt of the future of the Church concerning which they had the promise of the Lord that 'the gates of Hades shall not prevail against it' (Matt. xvi. 18), for he saw in it the body of Christ, whose life was guaranteed by His own immortality, and he knew that at the last He would present it to Himself 'a glorious church, holy and without blemish' (Eph. v. 27).

Chapter IV

THE CATHOLIC SCHEME

THE patristic Church was troubled by the growing contrast between the mediocre achievement and its declared aim of rearing a new humanity, and it became an urgent question how the situation was to be handled with due regard alike to the glory of God and the welfare of the flock. The Montanist sect, impressively represented by Tertullian, proposed to apply a drastic purge that would make of it a veritable communion of saints. In the following century Novatian led an influential party, the first to be called Puritan, which contended that it should permanently exclude from its membership those who apostatised under persecution or were guilty of adultery. Had Tertullian become Bishop of Carthage and Novatian Bishop of Rome, the policy might have prevailed for a season, but the Church would have sinned against mercy when it drove into the wilderness many who sincerely clung to the fold, while the beauty of its holiness would have been marred by spiritual pride and a growing fringe of hypocrisy. The decision was to take the optimistic view suggested by the Parable of the Leaven, and to follow the patient course enjoined in the Parable of the Tares. The holiness of the Church was an article of faith, but the working conception was that of the saving institution. It was not dismayed by the difficulty of changing the natural man, for it took courage to believe that its members were regenerated by an initial baptismal miracle, and continuously strengthened by the infusion of grace through additional sacramental channels. As fellow-worker with God, it addressed itself to the culture of souls on lines now familiar in education, separating its pupils into two divisions according to their talents and opportunities, prescribing to them a lower and a higher standard of attainment, and providing corresponding courses of instruction and training. To the main body, entangled as it was in secular life, a decent standard of piety and virtue was proposed as sufficient, while the select class was dedicated to the pursuit of perfection under the promising conditions of an unworldly environment and an ascetic mode of life. In both divisions sacraments were used as the chief means of grace, while all were incited to greater diligence by the prospect of rewards in proportion to their merits.

Approved in principle by the post-apostolic Church, this system was similarly elaborated in the East and in the West during the Middle Ages. It was attacked at the Reformation as containing, along with the gold of revelation, a large alloy of superstition and commercialism. It fell to the Roman Catholic Church to meet this indictment, and the Council of Trent expounded its position in 'decrees which are the utterance of jealous defence, and canons with their anathemas which are the challenge of proud defiance.'[1] When the attention of the Graeco-

[1] Curtis, *History of Creeds and Confessions of Faith*, 1911, p. 107.

Russian Church was drawn to the Augsburg Confession there were individuals, among them the patriarch Cyril Lucar, who sympathised with the evangelical principles, but the Synod of Jerusalem declared its emphatic agreement with Rome on the capital issues of sacramental efficacy and meritorious works.[1]

We proceed to consider the distinctive features of the Catholic scheme for the making and perfecting of the new creature.

I

THE GENESIS OF THE NEW MAN

The Catholic Church has ever emphasised that a man must be born again, and that it was only made possible by the redeeming work of Christ and the mission of the Holy Spirit. In the Pelagian controversy it anathematised the school which reduced the experience to a matter of improvement by teaching and example, and in the Middle Ages it was axiomatic even for rationalising scholastics that the Christian is a new creature supernaturally begotten and supernaturally nourished. The Council of Trent emphatically reaffirmed the necessity of the new birth, and its dependence on the divine initiative and provision. The cardinal blessing of the Gospel was set forth as justification, by which was primarily meant 'the sanctification and renewal of the inward man, through the voluntary reception of the grace, and of the gifts, whereby man of unjust becomes

---

[1] Schaff, *Creeds of Christendom*, i. pp. 61 ff.

just' (Sess. VI. 7). It is necessary, since 'men are born unjust, being propagated of the seed of Adam,' and 'if they were not born again in Christ they never would be made just' (Sess. VI. 3). The remission of sins was also included in justification, but on the footing that the divinely wrought sanctification is the ground of the remission of sins, and that the degree of sanctification attained is the measure of the benefits bestowed. 'The medicine whereby Christ cures our diseases,' so the theory has been fairly stated, 'is a divine spiritual quality which, received into the soul, doth first make it to be one of them who are born of God, and secondly endues it to bring forth such works as they do that are born of Him, maketh the soul gracious and amiable in the sight of God, washeth out all the stains and pollutions of sin, so that by it through the merit of Christ we are delivered as from sin so from eternal death the reward of sin.' [1] In brief, 'first sanctification then forgiveness' was the divinely appointed order in the appropriation of salvation. At the same time it was made clear that the affirmation of the priority of sanctification was far from implying that the sinner is called to attain by his own efforts to the goodness which merits the divine favour and obtains remission of sins. The faithful were given to dwell first in awe and gratitude on the many and necessary causes of justification on the side of God—'the final cause is the glory of God and of Jesus Christ, the efficient cause is a merciful God who washes and sanctifies gratuitously, the meritorious cause is His only begotten who

---

[1] Hooker, *Discourse of Justification*, 1850, ii. p. 603 (condensed).

when we were enemies merited justification by his most holy passion, and the formal cause is his justice by which we receive justice within us which the Holy Ghost distributes to every one as he wills' (Sess. VI. 7).

An indispensable function was attributed to Baptism as the means by which the new creature is brought into being. 'The instrumental cause of justification,' it was decreed, 'is the sacrament of baptism, which is the sacrament of faith, without which (faith) no man was ever justified' (*ibid.*). The effect of the sacrament is that 'putting on Christ, we are made thereby entirely a new creature obtaining a full and entire remission of all sins' (Sess. XIV. 2).

In treating of Baptism the Council of Trent chiefly concerned itself with the case of adults. Assuming an adequate preparation of the catechumens, it gave a detailed description of the model experience. 'Excited and assisted by divine grace,' it was said, 'they conceive faith by hearing, believing those things to be true which God has revealed and promised, they understand themselves to be sinners, and are profitably agitated by the fear of divine justice, they turn to consider the mercy of God, confiding that He will be propitious to them for Christ's sake, they begin to love Him as the fountain of all justice, and are therefore moved by a hatred and detestation of sins, when they purpose to receive baptism, to begin a new life and to keep the commandments of God' (Sess. VI. 6). But this was too high-pitched to be compulsory, and with support from earlier Popes it was held that it confers the promised grace on those who do not 'place an obstacle thereto' by wilful unbelief and impenitence (Sess. VII. 6). When the power of the sacrament was thus impeded it was supposed that it becomes dormant in the recipient, and that in the event of a change of heart it revives for the performance of the gracious work.

The doctrine of baptismal regeneration was a generalisation from the experience of one class of baptized adults. It was illustrated by Cyprian, who confessed that before baptism he was unconverted and did not even believe that such a change was possible. But 'after that by the help of the water of new birth,' he wrote, 'the stain of former years had been washed away, and a light from above, serene and pure, had been infused into my reconciled heart, that which had been born of the flesh and had been living in the practice of sins, began to be of God and was animated by the spirit of holiness.' [1] A second class sought baptism because they had already been regenerated. It was so with Augustine, who, after telling how he agonized over his sins, heard a call from God through His word, and resolved to 'put on the Lord Jesus Christ and make no provision for the flesh,' concluded with the testimony that 'God did then convert him to Himself.' Baptized some months later, he mentions as the additional benefit the assurance that his sins were completely washed away.[2] A third class, in some periods much the largest, consisted of persons who were not converted either at or before baptism, such as Roman

[1] *Epistles*, i. 4 (condensed). [2] *Confessions*, Bks. VIII., IX.

citizens of the age of Constantine who blindly followed the multitude, and the Frankish or Anglian soldiers who professed the faith out of loyalty to their earthly king. The term consecration might legitimately have been applied to cover these diverse baptismal experiences, but to call the whole mass the regenerate was to debase a great word, and to mislead many as to their actual standing with God.

Regeneration was also claimed for baptized infants on the ground that they offer no resistance to the infusion of grace. The Viennese Council decreed that baptism in the name of the triune God is 'the perfect saving remedy for children in common with adults,' and favoured the belief that through the sacrament children receive 'along with the remission of sins virtues and formative grace.' [1] The Tridentine pronouncement was that 'infants, who could not as yet commit any sins of themselves, are for this cause truly baptized for the remission of sins, that in them that may be cleansed away by regeneration which they have contracted by generation' (Sess. v. 4). The opinion was condemned that 'children after having received baptism are not to be reckoned among the faithful' (Sess. vii. of Baptism, 13), which implied that they also as 'justified received together with the remission of sins all these infused at once, faith, hope and charity.'

Infant baptism is amply justified by the practice of the early Church, supported as this was by the precedent of circumcision, and by the example of the Saviour who gave His blessing to little children.

---

[1] Denzinger, *Enchiridion*, 482-3.

It is a little faith which does not set great store on
the sacred ordinance in which the babe, with the
benefit of the intercession of the Church and of
believing parents, is dedicated to the heavenly
Father and placed in the keeping of the Good
Shepherd. We expect that a child with a good
ancestry will inherit some of the sterling qualities
of the stock, and there is reason for expecting a still
greater benefaction from the Father of Spirits when
it is bespoken by the prayer of faith. As a fact, in
every generation of the Christian era there have been
some who were manifestly sanctified from the cradle,
and it may well be believed that in some cases this
was God's baptismal gift. But to claim for all infants
a radical renewal by baptism is inconsistent with the
most patent facts, which rather confirm the theory of
the operation of a law of election within the economy
of grace.

II

The Ordinary Course

As a school of sanctification the Church was
assigned the task of building up the character of the
new man on the foundation laid in baptism. The
content of Christian character was summed up as
holiness and righteousness, and was expounded by
the scholastic divines as a synthesis of the virtues of
prudence, temperance, fortitude and justice with the
graces of faith, hope and charity. The methods
employed included attendance at public worship,
priestly guidance and correction, and the practice

of meditation and prayer with fasting at stated seasons. The special features were the value attached to the elaborated sacramental system, the extension of the range of heavenly friendship, and the strengthening of the moral dynamic by a doctrine of merit.

1. The pre-eminence of the sacraments among the means of grace was affirmed in the strongest terms. 'It is through the most holy sacraments,' it was declared, 'that all true justice begins, or being begun is increased, or being lost is repaired.' The number of the 'true and proper' sacraments was fixed at seven —Baptism, Confirmation, the Eucharist, Penance, Extreme Unction, Order and Matrimony (Sess. VII.).

Confirmation revives what was received in baptism, and is not a mere confession of faith, but brings an additional gift of the Holy Spirit (Sess. VII. 1). The Eucharist provides 'the spiritual food of souls whereby may be fed and strengthened those who live with his life who said 'he that eateth me, the same also shall live by me,' and 'is an antidote whereby we may be freed from daily faults, and be preserved from mortal sins' (Sess. XIII. 2). As the Mass it has the virtue of a propitiatory sacrifice, so that if we draw nigh unto Him with penitent hearts, 'God is appeased, forgiving even heinous sins and crimes, and that both to the faithful who are living and to those who are departed in Christ' (Sess. XXII. 2). Penance 'bestows a remedy of life on those who may after baptism have delivered themselves up to the servitude of sin and the power of the Devil.' It consists of three parts: contrition, which is 'a detestation of sin committed, with the purpose of not sinning in the future'; confession to

F

a priest, which is to be made at least once in the year; and satisfaction, whereby 'we are able through Jesus Christ to make satisfaction to God the Father by punishments voluntarily undertaken of ourselves for the punishment of sin, or by those imposed at the discretion of the priest, and also by the temporal scourges inflicted of God and patiently borne by us' (Sess. xiv. 8, 9). For the dying was provided Extreme Unction, which procures the blessings of the 'cleansing away sins if there be any still to be expiated, as also the remains of sin,' 'the raising up and strengthening of the soul of the sick person,' and even 'the recovery of bodily health when expedient for the welfare of the soul' (Sess. xiv.). A special sacramental provision was made for the two most important classes. Ordination separates the priest-hood from the laity by conferring on them a special enduement of grace, and in particular by deliver-ing to them 'the power of consecrating offering and administering Christ's body and blood, as also of forgiving and of retaining sins' (Sess. xxiii. 1). Matrimony joins together the man and the woman in a union that may only be dissolved by death, and bestows on them 'the grace by which natural love is perfected' (Sess. xxiv.). Of these sacraments are Baptism, Confirmation and Order, which imprint an indelible character, and may not be repealed. The Eucharist is invested with a unique dignity, since 'the other sacraments have then first the power of sanctifying when they are used, whereas in the Eucharist, before being used, there is the Author himself of sanctity' (Sess. xiii. 3).

The sacraments were magnified by making it an article of faith that they confer grace 'by the work performed' upon those 'who do not impose an obstacle thereunto.' By this was meant that they have an efficacy like to that of natural agents or of tools on which we rely to do a certain work provided they are not thwarted by adverse factors. Their action was illustrated by the fire which consumes material on condition that it is combustible, and by the carpenter's saw which cuts the rough plank of wood if not stopped by some harder substance.[1] At the same time it was left to theologians to debate as to how much is to be attributed to a virtue implanted in the sacraments, how much to the direct action of Him to whom when rightly used they make an effective appeal for the bestowal of promised grace.

The original sacraments are a precious part of the common good of Christendom, and there was obvious need of ordinances of the kind which were linked with Baptism and the Lord's Supper under the name of sacraments, and which were preserved in modified forms and with some changes of name in the great Protestant Churches. But there still remains the question as to the due place and proportion of sacramental machinery in the Christian economy, and it is difficult to defend the prominence given to it in the Catholic system save by the plea that it was necessary to recast the Gospel in this form in order to give to the faithful the most realising sense of God, and stimulate them to greater zeal in good works. There

[1] Thomas Aquinas, *Summa*, III. Qu. 62, Art. IV. Bellarmine, *Opera*, 721, Tom. III. ii. 1.

are passages in the Gospels and the Epistles in which, when allowance is not made for figures of speech, the highest sacramental teaching may be found, but the significant fact is that while every vital aspect of the Christian revelation is the special theme of one or other of the New Testament writers, there is no canonical book which sets forth Christianity as the religion of the ordered distribution of sacramental grace through the mediation of a human priesthood. And when this was done by the Church itself it was unjustifiable to require belief in the miracle of transubstantiation of those who sought communion with the Lord at His table. Moreover, the value of the original sacraments and of the kindred ordinances was seriously impaired when it was taught that they confer grace 'by the work performed,' and that it is sufficient if the recipient does not offer resistance. The Scriptural analogy is the action of food, not that of the fire or of the saw, and as it is required of the body that it actively participates by the acceptance and assimilation of the food, so is it required of the soul that it lays hold by faith on Christ and His benefits. In the theological schools it was explained that the sacraments do not operate in magical fashion, but the popular impression was otherwise, and the doctrine and practice disposed the unspiritual to trust in them rather than in the Saviour for the forgiveness of sins and the title to Heaven.

2. The faithful were encouraged to seek additional help by cultivating the friendship of secondary powers of the heavenly world.

Much importance was attached to the ministry of

angels, for which there is a very substantial basis in Scripture (Heb. i. 14). Their special concern was conceived to be the protection and furtherance of the interests of the Church, while nations also were bidden to look to an angelic patron with the character of their good genius. The individual was comforted with the vision of a guardian angel who protects him from dangers to body and soul, conveys and supports his prayers, and will be with him in the valley of the shadow of death.[1] The Virgin Mary was exalted to semi-divine rank, and her sympathy and help were confidently bespoken for suffering humanity. In a sense, it was said, we owe to her our redemption, inasmuch as her consent was needed in order to the assumption of human nature by the eternal Son. She even ranks as our co-redeemer since 'nothing is obtained from the treasury of grace save by the will of God through Mary,' and just as none can come to the Father but by the Son, so may it be said that none can come to the Son but by the Mother.[2]

The saints in glory 'present the prayers of believers to God,' and because of their merits they have power with God and prevail. At the same time it was made clear that the adoration of the saints differs in kind from the worship of God, and that its ultimate meaning is that it redounds to the glory of the Lord to whom we owe all.[3]

There should be no difficulty about the existence of angels, as the universe is a realm of graded excellence, and even as man with his rational

---

[1] Bartmann, *Dogmatik*, 1928, vol. i. p. 263.
[2] Denzinger, *op. cit.*, 1940a.   [3] *Op. cit.*, 342.

and moral endowment rises above the animals, so doubtless also are there orders of spiritual beings with degrees of dignity and power intermediate between humanity and godhead. We do well to think about glorified saints, among whom the Virgin Mary has a unique place, and there is better reason for desiring their help than for beseeching a friend who is a better Christian than ourselves to remember us in his prayers. The fatal objection to the invocation of angels and saints is that we have no assurance that our voice will reach those whom we address, or even that they have any knowledge of us, and the wise course is to address our prayers to the omniscient God, leaving it to Him to make use of His instruments, which may well include guardian angels, for carrying out His gracious purposes with His children.

3. The moral dynamic was strengthened by the doctrine of Purgatory, which made the faithful more afraid to offend and come short. When the Gospel was preached to pagans the fear of hell led many to seek safety in believing, but it lost most of its terrors for those who were born into Christian homes, and who were given to believe that, unless they were cast out as incorrigible, their calling and election were sure. It was therefore taught by Origen, and eventually made an article of faith, that 'the souls of those who depart in the fear of God before making satisfactions by fruits worthy of repentance for sins of omission and of commission are purified after death by the punishments of Purgatory.' Their sufferings were nevertheless alleviated by the

---

[1] Council of Florence. Denzinger, *op. cit.*, 693.

prayers and the pious gifts of the living as well as by an angelic ministry, and it was said that there is more of God's sunshine in Purgatory than on earth, since its discipline is favourable to growth in grace, and the purification is a pledge of the Father's good pleasure to give them the Kingdom (Sess. xxv.).

There seems to be a suggestion of some such state in the saying of Jesus about degrees of punishment (Luke xx. 47), and in the apostolic warning that 'the fire will prove each man's work,' and 'if his work be burned, he shall suffer loss: but he himself shall be saved' (1 Cor. iii. 15). But there is a notable parsimony of revelation in this field, and the doctrine of Purgatory was at best a commonsense addition that was calculated to be useful. It is natural to suppose that the average Christian is not fit for Heaven when he leaves this world, or wicked enough to be consigned to eternal torments; and it seemed to be all for their good that such should be given to believe that though safe for eternity they had to reckon at the next stage with retributive justice.

The faithful were also stimulated to greater zeal in good works by the promise of rewards proportionate to their merits. The meritorious acts included prayers and masses, gifts and legacies to the Church as the representative of Christ, works of mercy in the form of almsgiving and personal service, and also the patient endurance of the ills to which flesh is heir. The rewards on which most stress was laid were spiritual blessing—'increase of grace, eternal life, and if so be that one depart in grace an increase of glory in heaven'; but there was also the promise of

the temporal blessings of health and prosperity 'in so
far as favourable to progress in the divine life'
(Sess. vi. 16).

The prominence thus given to a doctrine of merit
and recompense is intelligible from the practical point
of view. Much has been made of the principle in
education, and in the work of the world it is found that
men make the fullest use of their powers when it is
known that the profit and the honour will be proportionate to their services. And the Church doubtless
thought that in this matter it had something to learn
from the children of this world. At the same time
it warned the faithful that though much was attributed
to good works it did not mean that a Christian should
trust and glory in himself and not in the Lord ' whose
bounty is so great that he will have the things which
are his own gifts to be their merits' (Sess. vi. 16).
There was also a reminder that human offerings are
for the most part congruous merits, which merely
meant conditions of receiving divine blessings, and
therefore gave no more ground for boasting than
the qualifications which entitle indigent persons to
the benefits of a charity. At the same time it clung
tenaciously to the ambiguous and provocative term,
as the idea of merit was embodied in its fundamental
principle of the priority of sanctification to acceptance
with God. This principle, as we shall see later, was
open to grave objection on religious grounds, but the
doctrine of merits was zealously reaffirmed because
it was a safeguard against the deadly error that the
divine favour can be enjoyed without righteousness,
and also because its abandonment would have

shattered the system which was a chief source of its influence.

III

THE WAY OF PERFECTION

With the growth of the primitive Church, as was observed, it seemed that a high level of sanctity was unattainable by the general body of its members, involved as they also were in the life of social and economic groups that are dominated by the self-seeking spirit of the world. Yet it might not be forgotten that Jesus said, 'ye shall be perfect, as your heavenly Father is perfect' (Matt. v. 48). It was therefore a natural inference that this pointed to the formation of a class consecrated to a higher ideal, even as Jesus bade some leave home and calling and make their own concern the things of the Kingdom of God. In the apostolic age the precedent was so far followed by setting apart chosen brethren to a branch of the work of the ministry, which claimed them for disinterested service, and also promoted their sanctification in the measure in which they were found faithful. Among the laity there arose a hunger and thirst after perfection which it was sought to reach in still more complete detachment from the world. The movement began in Egypt with a multitude that followed Paul and Anthony into the desert, where they lived in the first instance as hermits and later in ascetic communities. When it spread in adjacent lands it became subject to the Rule of St. Basil, which, in the words of the Roman Breviary, 'effected a noble synthesis of the contemplative and

the active life.' Still more stress was laid on the
spiritual profit of labour in the Benedictine Rule,
which during the Middle Ages was largely normative
for the monastic life of Western Christendom. The
way of perfection was opened to women in sisterhoods
that offered the privilege of a sheltered piety, while
feminine devotion was also guided into Christlike
ministration to the sick and the poor.

The aim of the monastic system was to carry on the
new man to perfection. The mortification of the
natural man was promoted by the vows of poverty,
chastity and obedience, whereby, as St. Thomas
explains, mortal blows were struck at avarice,
sensuality and pride, the bosom sins of the child of
Adam.[1] The hardest to subdue, it appeared, was
pride, which might rather be fostered by dwelling on
the merit of the great renunciation, and humility was
magnified as the crowning evidence of the translation
from death to life. It was compared to the ladder in
Jacob's dream that reached to heaven, and the steps
were said to be twelve—'to live ever in the fear of God,
to seek ever to do the will of God, to obey the superior
as the representative of God, to endure injuries meekly,
to confess to the superior all evil thoughts and actions,
to perform without murmur menial and painful tasks,
to think of oneself as a worm and no man, to do
nothing contrary to regulations and good example, to
bridle the tongue, to be slow to laugh, to be gentle
and grave in discourse and sparing of words, to be
humble in heart as well as in speech and behaviour.'[2]

---

[1] Thomas Aquinas, *op. cit.*, II. I. Qu. 108, Art. IV.
[2] *Benedictine Rule*, chap. vii.

By the self-effacing vows the house might be emptied
and swept, but it was needful that if the evil spirits
returned they should find God in possession. The
primary aim, therefore, was to cultivate a constant
sense of the divine presence, and to bring a man to
love God with all his heart and soul and strength
and mind. The Benedictine monks rose after mid-
night for the prolonged devotions of Vigils, at day-
break Matins claimed another hour, after the morning
meal and before going to work there was a meeting
for prayer, in the midst of their labours they came
together at intervals to remember God, at sunset
there was the longer Service of Vespers, and after
supper and before they retired to rest the day was
rounded off by the office of Compline. On Sundays
and other holy days the Eucharist was administered
as the chiefest aid to sanctity. If for many this
ceaseless round of worship was a weariness to the
flesh, in some souls it awakened a greater hunger and
thirst for God. 'Throughout its career we find
Monasticism upholding the ideal of direct intercourse
of the soul with its Maker, and it is to the monasteries
that we must turn for the rise of the mystics.' [1] It was
in accordance with the mystical technique when the
monks were bound to the way of purification and the
way of contemplation, and the most devout were
disposed to go on to the crowning experience of a
vital union with the Infinite Being. Popes were alive
to the danger of misconceiving this union, and it was
condemned as an impious opinion 'that we are

[1] *Benedictine Rule*, chap. vii. Workman, *Evolution of the Monastic
Ideal*, 1913, p. 344.

wholly transformed into God even as in the sacrament
the host is transformed into the body of Christ, and
that whatever God the Father has given to His only
Son in human nature He has given to us.' [1]

The commandment to love our neighbour was
made increasingly explicit in the programme of the
later foundations. Love of the brethren was promoted
by modelling the institution on the family-circle
which has an authoritative and honoured head, and
whose members have common possessions, eat and
drink together, co-operate in the tasks of the household, and bear one another's burdens. The staple
occupation was horticulture and agriculture, with the
practice of the allied crafts, and it was on the initiative
or under the guidance of the monks that, throughout
wide regions of Europe, forests were felled and waste
lands transformed into rich pastures and fertile fields.
Learning was held in honour, and it was to the
monasteries that the nascent nations of the West
largely owed the preservation of the literary treasures
of Rome and Greece, the tutoring of talented youth,
and the impetus to the founding of Universities.
Monks also played no small part, both as patrons and
fellow-workers, in the progress of the arts of archi-
tecture, painting and sculpture. The works of mercy
named by Christ were included in the programme.
Above all, it was the monasteries that took to heart
the command to go into all the world and preach
the Gospel to every creature, for they inspired and
sent forth evangelists who completed the Christian
conquest of Europe, and did much planting and

---

[1] Denzinger, *op. cit.*, 510-11.

watering while as yet territorial Churches were in their infancy. When in the Dark Ages there was a call for new methods of aggression on a world lying in wickedness, Francis of Assisi founded an Order of Friars who renounced the sheltered home for a vagrant and mendicant life to the end that, though at much peril to their own souls, they might preach from city to city, and take by the hand the chiefest of sinners and the poorest of the poor.

The monastery can well be defended in principle as a special school of spiritual culture. It was of the genus of a social club, and combining as it did a deeply religious atmosphere with manual labour and scholarly and artistic interests, it ranks high above the secular counterpart in which the main concern is with the politics and the gossip of the day and the fortunes of the card-table. Specialisation is necessary in every secular sphere; it has rightly been claimed in the religious sphere for the clergy, and it seems desirable that devout laymen who hear no call to the work of the ministry should be able to give themselves to a mode of life favourable to constant and close communion with God, and calling for utterly self-denying service of man. The only question is whether in binding himself to poverty, celibacy and obedience, the monk took the safest route towards his professed goal of perfection. For the ordinary man diligence in a useful calling is the surest way of showing love of his neighbour, wealth indefinitely increases his power of doing good, marriage is not only a normal duty to society but a protection against a turbulent impurity of mind and heart, and there is reason to think that the dignity of a child of God forbids him to promise unconditional obedience to an ecclesiastical superior. But it is also true that it is left to the good Christian to decide under what conditions he may best rise to the height of his calling, and those who vow themselves to poverty, celibacy and obedience for Christ's sake may not be severely censured when it is remembered how many professing Christians squander their wealth on luxury and display, resolve on celibacy merely because it pleases them, and blindly obey the dictates of their social circle or the stronger characters among their friends. The tragic mistake was that in course of time the conditions of entrance were made too easy, and the necessary steps were not taken to preserve the purity of the institution. Had the monasteries been much fewer in number, the probation longer, and the vows subject to recall, with a recurring purge after the manner of Gideon, they might well have endured as an abiding source of inspiration and strength to the Church in its service of the world.

The Catholic scheme of spiritual culture was based on revelation and a profound study of human nature, and was worked out with a signal combination of faith and practical sagacity. And great things have been accomplished by it. It meant much for the Western peoples destined to be in the van of civilisation that they entered an ecclesiastical school which taught a sublime doctrine of God linked with a high-souled ethic, instead of being starved by a discredited pagan creed and honouring the principles of a tribal morality. Its influence penetrated the life of the Western nations, and in every Christian country there were many of every social class to whom it gave a deep-seated sense of God, and of the obligation to please Him by ceasing to do evil and learning to do well. In addition to this leavening process, conversions have continuously taken place under Catholic training of the radical kind in which God or His Christ becomes the centre and sun of the inner life, and gives the law for work in the world. An Italian psychologist assures us that conversions still take place in the Roman communion much more deserving of the name than those reported in Protestant studies of the experience.[1] Literature old and new has portraits of priests radiant with holiness and self-sacrificing devotion, and it was the glory of the monasteries, as was already observed, that they produced convincing and constraining examples of the life that is hid with Christ in God, and of the spiritual service in which it issues.

There was, however, a measure of shortcoming and failure which in every age was grievous and shameful when judged by the divine standard, and in some periods was felt to be scandalous from the human point of view of decency and consistency. In the ninth and again in the twelfth century the situation was very evil, and though it was improved by a quickening from on high and the new work of new missionary orders, at the close of the Middle Ages there was a flowing tide of unbelief and wickedness, and the chosen seats of sanctity were being captured by the powers of the world and the flesh. In such circumstances it was natural to suspect that there was some-

[1] De Sanctis, *Religious Conversion*, 1927, p. 34.

thing radically wrong in the methods by which the Christian salvation had been applied, and it seemed to many that the system should be recast in accordance with a different principle. The uprising against the Catholic system was fostered by other motives— among them dislike of priestly intrusion into family life, a desire for the liberation of the truth-seeking mind from ecclesiastical censorship, and, not least, jealousy of the power and envy of the wealth of the Church to which the sacerdotal claims and the sacramental machinery so largely contributed. But the driving power of the reforming movement came from the depths of man's spiritual and moral being, for the Reformers testified that they had recovered from the Scriptures the Gospel of justification by faith which gave a better assurance of the forgiveness of sins by a gracious God, and at the same time a better guarantee of the power needed for serving Him in newness of life.

CHAPTER V

THE EVANGELICAL SCHEME

THE basis of the evangelical scheme was the Christian faith as set forth in the ancient Creeds. For the Reformers it was axiomatic that God became man that men may be renewed in the image of God, and that the needed provision was made in the redeeming work of the Son and the sanctifying mission of the Holy Spirit. The religious issues in the controversy chiefly concerned the manner in which the benefits of the great salvation are conveyed from above and appropriated from below. Catholicism and Evangelicalism might be described as two schools of spiritual therapeutics which, while cognate, differed as to the order of events in the cure of sin-stricken souls, and also as to the precise service rendered in the treatment by the several means of grace. Within the evangelical school, also, differences developed that were deemed of such importance as to involve a separation into Lutheran and Reformed Churches. These were, however, at one in their Confessions in witnessing to the gospel of justification by faith as the miracle of divine wisdom whereby the sinner in being restored to the favour of God is concurrently equipped as a new creature. At the Reformation this recovered gospel was confirmed by a demonstration of the Spirit and of power which resulted in the conversion of

G

many individuals and in the leavening of the life of
nations by lofty religious and moral ideals. The
fruits, nevertheless, fell far short of the original
expectations, and in the generations following there
were powerful ecclesiastical parties which sought to
improve the situation by supplementing the evangelical scheme on rigorist, ritualistic and humanistic
lines. In the eighteenth century there took place a
widespread evangelical revival in which it was again
seen that the gospel of justification by faith when
proclaimed with burning conviction, and seconded by
a movement of the Spirit in the spirit of an age, is
an unequalled instrument for the transformation of
the natural man.

I

The Fundamental Principle

The principle of the evangelical scheme was the
necessity of justification by faith as the decisive
beginning and the persisting accompaniment of the
new life.

1. The cardinal boon of the Christian salvation, as
in the Catholic system, was termed the justification
of the sinner. But the term primarily meant for the
Catholic that the unjust being is made just or
sanctified, for the evangelical that he is accepted as
just or pardoned. It was as if a minister and a
lawyer were discussing a criminal case, when one
chiefly thought of what might be done to reform a
bad character, the other of how he might be acquitted
in an impending trial. But the contest for the

possession of a word pointed to a vital conflict of theory as to the order of procedure in the salvation of souls. The Catholic order was: first, sanctification on the divine initiative and by the help of divine grace; then, forgiveness on the ground, and in proportion to the degree, of the goodness bestowed and attained. The evangelical order was: first, forgiveness on the sole condition of a heartfelt trust in the mercy of God in Christ; then, a progressive sanctification by the Holy Spirit whose help is the confirming gift of the reconciled Father. They are illustrated by the two ways in which a penitent prodigal may be treated: one to assure him of restoration to the family circle when he shall have made good, the other to help him to make good by letting bygones be bygones and encouraging him in a fresh start.

It was emphasised in all the Confessions that justification primarily means that the sinner is accepted as righteous, or acquitted, and this not on the ground of any goodness of his own, but because of the merits of the Saviour. 'They teach,' the Lutheran article runs, 'that men cannot be justified before God by their own powers, merits or works, but are justified freely for Christ's sake through faith, when they believe they are received into favour, and their sins forgiven for Christ's sake, who by His death hath satisfied for our sins.' [1] The Anglican Symbol made it clearer that in this context justification means being 'accounted righteous before God,' and emphasised that we are so accepted 'only for the merit of our

[1] Augsburg Confession, Pt. I., Art. IV.

Lord and Saviour, Jesus Christ, by faith, and not for our own works or deservings.'[1] 'Justification,' the Calvinist was taught, 'is an act of God's free grace, wherein He pardoneth all our sins, and accepteth us as righteous in His sight, only for the righteousness of Christ imputed to us and received by faith alone.'[2]

If the doctrine of justification by faith were not a revealed truth it would still rank as an intuition of spiritual genius, for in solving the capital religious problem it concurrently solves the capital moral problem of the human lot. The crux of the religious situation is how man, notwithstanding his black record of sinful actions, and his evil dispositions, may hope to gain and keep the favour of the all-holy God. It is the common faith of Christians that God Himself prepared the way when He 'so loved the world that he gave his only begotten Son' (John. iii. 16), and that 'there is now no condemnation to them that are in Christ Jesus' (Rom. viii. 1). And the Catholic Church gave an added sense of security when it promised the divine favour and eternal salvation to those who were of its household, made use of the quickening sacraments, and sought to perform the good works which God has made possible by the help of His grace. But the faithful had still much reason to tremble when they were given to know that at every stage their standing with God depended on the degree in which they had become just, and that notwithstanding the meritorious works which they might plead there were outstanding debts that fell to

---

[1] Thirty-Nine Articles, Art. XI.
[2] Westminster Shorter Catechism, Q. 33.

be discharged by temporal punishments and in the torments of purgatory. For an age in which judgment to come was as certain as death, it was therefore glad tidings indeed that there is full forgiveness for the sinner here and hereafter when he throws himself on the mercy of God, relying only on the merits of the Saviour who made atonement for his sins and fulfilled all righteousness. The comfort of the doctrine was much prized for itself, and also as evidence that the evangelical message was the truth of God. 'Godly and fearful consciences,' the Lutheran contended, 'cannot be quieted by any works, but by faith alone, when they believe assuredly that they have a God who is propitiated for Christ's sake.' [1] 'When one has regard to his own righteousness,' said Calvin, 'his pitiful cry is "Oh wretched man that I am," but he triumphs gloriously over life and death and all accusation when he flees to the righteousness which rests on the divine mercy alone.' [2] The Anglican Confession claims for the doctrine that 'we are justified by faith only,' that 'it is most wholesome and very full of comfort.' [3]

The ethical problem is how the natural man, with his inheritance of carnal and worldly propensities, is to be brought to render obedience to the exacting laws of the all-holy God. And the evangelical solution was that when the sinner seeks first the divine favour and pardon, righteousness will be added unto him. He is like unto a man digging for hid treasure, who has the double reward of unearthing the treasure and

[1] Augsburg Confession, Pt. I. Art. XX.   [2] *Institutio*, iii. 11.
[3] Thirty-Nine Articles, Art. XI.

fertilising his field. The gift of the Holy Spirit follows, Luther explained, if we have truly had faith in Christ, when ' our hearts are renewed and put on new affections, so that they are able to bring forth good works.' [1] 'Distinguished in thought,' said Calvin, 'justification and the new birth are joined together by an indissoluble bond, and Christ justifies none whom He does not also sanctify.' [2] The Anglican statement was that 'good works, albeit that they follow after justification, do spring necessarily of a true faith, insomuch that by them a lively faith may be as evidently known as a tree is discerned by its fruits.' [3]

2. The gospel of justification by faith had two corollaries which impinged on the existing sacramental and sacerdotal system.

If the one indispensable condition of acceptance with God is faith in Christ, and if 'belief cometh of hearing,' it follows that the primary means of grace is ' the enlightening and convincing word of God.' Luther spoke of it as the pipe by which the Holy Spirit is poured into the heart, as the life-giving stream, and as the seed without which there can be no fruits.[4] 'God grants His Spirit or grace to no one,' it was declared, 'except with or through the preceding outward word,' and this was directed both against the enthusiasts 'who boasted that they had the Spirit without and before the word,' and against the Pope 'who boasts that all laws exist in the shrine of his

[1] Augsburg Confession, Pt. I. Art. XX.
[2] *Institutio*, iii. 16.
[3] Art. XII.
[4] Kostlin, *Luthers Theologie*, 1863, vol. ii. p. 56.

heart even though it be above and contrary to the Scripture.'[1] The most conspicuous assertion of the primacy of the word was made by the Reformed Churches which gave the pulpit precedence over the communion table, and were more concerned about the acoustics than about the beauty of the sanctuary. Fastening on Augustine's description of the sacraments as 'the visible word,' the Reformers stressed as their function that they 'not only quicken but confirm faith in them that use them.'[2] They are also seals which guarantee the authenticity of the gracious promises made in the name of the Almighty. It could further be affirmed that they apply the blessings which they signify. The word of God in Scripture consists of the audible signs called language, while yet they are made by the Spirit to be 'the power of God unto salvation to every one that believeth'; and similarly it could be said that by the visible word of the Lord's Supper 'the worthy receivers are made partakers of His body and blood with all His benefits to their spiritual nourishment and growth in grace.'[3] The one substantial issue was whether the partaking of Christ in the sacrament meant that a benefit not otherwise bestowed is obtained by the corporeal act of eating and drinking. And on this question it was more and more left to the Reformed Churches strictly so-called, to maintain Luther's original view that he who has saving faith possesses Christ in the fulness of his benefits, and that therefore there remains

[1] Kostlin, *op. cit.* p. 249.
[2] Thirty-Nine Articles, Art. XXV. Augsburg Confession, Art. XIII.
[3] Westminster Shorter Catechism, Q. 96.

no unique and superlative gift to be added unto him.

The other offending corollary was the tenet of the priesthood of all believers. The office historically ascribed to a priest is to mediate between God and man; but in the matter of his justification the sinner needs no mediation save that of the heavenly High Priest, and when justified he obtains the full rights of a child of God, including free access to His presence at all times and in all places. 'They that are justified,' said Luther, 'are priests for that they are worthy to appear before God, to pray for one another, and to teach one another about God.'[1] It was indeed strongly emphasised that there is a spiritual division of labour under which the clerical class is charged with the administration of the word and sacraments, but it was on the footing that the proximate source of their commission is the priestly community of believers. The tenet was anathema to the Roman Catholic Church as it seriously menaced the prestige and the influence of the clerical office, and in particular reduced the sacrament of penance, even when a form of confession and absolution were retained, to a shadow of its former self. The evangelical defence was that apostles expressly taught the universal priesthood (1 Pet. ii. 5; Rev. i. 6), and that the doctrine gave good promise of arousing in the laity a deeper sense of responsibility, and claiming from them more abundant service, both in their homes and in the world, of the cause and Kingdom of God.

[1] Kostlin, *op. cit.*, vol. i. p. 316.

II

THE CONVERSION EXPERIENCE

While it was made clear that a man is not justified because of any merit he has acquired, it was equally insisted that he is not justified without being radically changed. Conversion had therefore a prominent place in evangelical teaching and preaching. In the first period the term was sometimes limited to repentance, sometimes extended to cover the whole process of renewal, but it came to be generally applied to the conjoined experience of repentance unto life and saving faith, when it could be identified with regeneration. An intensive study of the psychology of conversion was made by the later Lutheran divines. Repentance was analysed into a knowledge of sin, a sense of the divine wrath, agony of conscience, humiliation before God, sincere confession and hatred of sin.[1] Two strands of saving faith were distinguished: intellectual assent to the truths of Christianity, and the act of will by which the sinner throws himself on the divine mercy and puts his trust in the Saviour. There was also much discussion of the motives leading to conversion. The practical question which emerged, and over which a violent controversy raged, was whether the evangelist should seek to bring sinners to repentance by putting them in fear of the wrath of God, or by teaching them to love Him for His goodness. In a pastoral letter which Luther endorsed, Melanchthon instructed ministers that they should

[1] Gerhard, *Loci Theologici*, 1639, Tom. iii. de Poenitentia, cap. xi.

proclaim to men that under the Law, which requires a perfect obedience, they stand utterly condemned, and that there is a fearful looking for of judgment both in time and in eternity. The same procedure was approved by the Reformed Churches strictly so-called, though with the proviso that there is no true or perfected repentance until there is an apprehension of the mercy of God in Christ.[1] In the Presbyterian Churches, and the Puritanical school of the Church of England, the theory was zealously put into practice. The conversion-experience was popularised by Bunyan in the form of a perilous pilgrimage from the City of Destruction by way of the Slough of Despond and the thunders of Sinai to the place of the cross and the sepulchre where the burden of sin was rolled away. In sermons it was set forth in the form of a prosecution ending in an acquittal, and an outline of the proceedings may be profitably reproduced from a Puritan classic.

The accused is the careless sinner. He may be a nominal believer, a church-goer and an amiable person, but his hours are divided between his amusements and his business, and he does not give one hour's serious consideration to religion. Through the reading, and especially the preaching of the Word, he is awakened to the fact that this is a matter of tremendous importance. The preacher, speaking for God, arraigns him as a rebel against the Sovereign Majesty. He is charged with a persistent transgression of the divine laws, not perhaps by gross immorality, but at least by pride, sensual passion, worldliness, waste of time and talents, murmuring and repining. He has also been ungrateful for divine favours, has resisted the Holy Spirit and has been unfaithful to his solemn vows. There are in truth thousands

[1] Calvin, *Institutio*, iii. 3.

in Hell whose guilt was less than his. He pleads that he had a pious upbringing, that he knows the doctrines and the precepts of religion, that he has a fair moral character, that he was unaware of the gravity of his offences, and further that he was forced by a necessity of his nature to do things which are charged against him as crimes. But in his heart he knows that there is no valid defence, and that he is righteously doomed to death and everlasting torment. His one ray of hope is that, as he is still spared, the gates of mercy are not closed. He has some confused idea of a possible way of escape, and light comes when he is instructed that Christ suffered in his room and stead, and that His perfect righteousness is imputed to the sinner who clings to Him by faith. He resolves to trust in the Saviour, when he finds pardon and peace in believing, with an inward witness of his acceptance with God. Coincidently with his justification he receives a baptism of the Holy Spirit which makes of him a new creature with a divine disposition, even the mind which was in Christ Jesus. The engagement to be the Lord's is registered by a written pledge, and is sealed at the holy table.[1]

At the Reformation the Lutheran Agricola protested against attempting to drive sinners into the Kingdom by the terrors of the Law, and maintained they should be won by dwelling first and last on the depth of the riches of the love of God. In later periods a growing evangelical school has agreed with him, founding on the sayings that 'the goodness of God leadeth thee to repentance' (Rom. ii. 4), and that 'we love, because he first loved us' (1 John iv. 19). As a fact, there have ever been those who, unmoved by the menace of judgment, have been apprehended and constrained by the vision of love and sacrifice in the Godhead. That a true conversion, and even its fairest form, can be produced in this way was recog-

[1] Doddridge, *Rise and Progress of Religion in the Soul* (condensed).

nised by the other school. 'We are not to speak of the work of the Law,' said an orthodox Scottish evangelist, 'as if none might lay claim to God's favour who hath not had the preparatory work in the several stages of it, for the Lord doth not always keep that path with them. Some are brought to Christ in a sovereign way when the Lord by some few words of love doth take a person prisoner at the first, as He did Zacchaeus, and we have no word of a law-work dealing with them before they close with Jesus.' [1] The only question is which of the two methods is the better for awakening the unregenerate multitude out of their indifference, and whether the more effective can be honestly employed. Ritschl has reproached Melanchthon for an unworthy accommodation of the Gospel message to the limitations of 'the vulgar mind' when he advised preachers to begin with the terrors of the Law.[2] But fear is a powerful dynamic, and it is not contemptible but laudable to make men afraid when there is good reason for fear. A community is given to dread the approach of an epidemic to the end that it may take the necessary precautions against it, and it may be similarly thought that it is the duty of an institution which believes it, to give sinners to fear sin as the deadliest of maladies, to the end that in their perilous plight they may seek protection and healing in the gospel of the forgiveness of sins and of renovation by the Holy Spirit.

[1] Guthrie, *Saving Interest*, chap. ii. (condensed).
[2] *Rechtfertigung und Versöhnung*, 1874, vol. i. p. 188.

III

THE PROCESS OF SANCTIFICATION

Justified by faith and therewith regenerated, the Christian goes on to sanctification, pledged to the loftiest ideal and supplied with the necessary powers.

1. The Reformers disliked the scholastic definitions of the Christian ideal as too much coloured by philosophy and vitiated by their exaltation of the contemplative above the active life. They preferred to set forth the ideal in the form of an exposition of the Ten Commandments and of New Testament passages in which the perfected law was summarised in a Gospel setting. Taking for his text 'though I was free from all, I brought myself under bondage to all' (1 Cor. ix. 19), Luther named as the essential marks of the new life the freedom which is obtained by faith, and the self-renouncing service of God and man to which he dedicates himself under the inspiration of love.[1] Perfection, it was insisted, is furthered in the divine institution of the married state, and is compatible with a secular calling.[2] Calvin found the full programme in the passage which speaks of the grace of God as 'instructing us, to the intent that, denying ungodliness and worldly lusts, we should live soberly and righteously and godly in this present world' (Titus ii. 12). 'All the doings of our life,' he observes, 'are here brought into three parts, sobriety, righteousness and godliness. Sobriety

---

[1] *Von der Freiheit eines Christenmenschen,* 1520.
[2] Augsburg Confession, Pt. II. Art. I.

signifieth besides chastity and temperance a pure and sparing use of temporal things, and a patient suffering of poverty. Righteousness consists in giving to every man his own. Godliness severeth us from the defilings of the world, and with true holiness joineth us to God.' In the forefront was placed the duty of enthroning God as the sovereign ruler of the soul. 'The vital matter is that we should forsake self and dedicate ourselves to God. We are not our own, let us therefore forget ourselves and the things that are our own. We are God's, let us therefore live and die unto Him, leaving it to His wisdom and will to govern all our doings.' [1]

2. As the reconciled child of God the convert sets out on his new course with a great stimulus and a rich endowment. He has not only a constraining sense of gratitude, but knows himself a son of the heavenly Father, is knit in mystical union with the glorified Christ, and is strengthened and comforted by the gifts of the Holy Spirit. His part is to make diligent use of the word, sacraments and prayer, to serve God by diligence in his vocation, and also to become more Christlike by sharing, according to his ability, in the works of Christ.

It was a common reproach against the Reformers that they made religion popular by making it easy. As Dryden put it—

> Religion frights us with a mien severe;
> 'Tis prudence to reform her into ease,
> And put her in undress to make her please :
> A lively faith will bear aloft the mind,
> And leave the luggage of good works behind.[2]

---

[1] *Institutio*, iii. 7.   [2] *The Hind and the Panther*, iii.

generation, and again in Covenanting times, the attempt was made, though with dwindling success and conviction, to carry out the drastic programme.

2. The policy increasingly favoured in the Lutheran and Anglican Churches was to strengthen the hands of the ministry in the cure of souls by a higher valuation of sacramental means of grace. Luther clung to a high doctrine which included the baptismal regeneration of infants and the bodily presence of Christ in the Eucharist, and Confirmation and Penance, though not accepted as sacraments in the full sense, were retained as sufficiently authorised by Scripture and by their proved spiritual profit. The Anglican Reformers, notably Cranmer, Latimer and Cartwright, sat at Calvin's feet, and in the first period 'the battlemented stronghold of Calvinism towered aloft and dominated the Church.' [1] In the following generation it was widely held, as against the Puritans, 'that the Church of England before the Reformation and the Church of England after the Reformation were as much the same Church as a garden before it is weeded and after it is weeded.' [2] The sacraments were increasingly magnified in comparison with the preaching of the word, while yet the teaching of Andrewes and Laud about Baptism and the Eucharist was of a lower type than that of the contemporary Lutheran divines. On the other hand, sacerdotalism was held in check in Germany more than in England by the recognition of the principle of the universal priesthood.

[1] Dowden, *Theological Literature of the Church of England*, 1897, p. 67.
[2] Bramhall, *Works*, 1677, vol. i. p. 101.

3. With the waning of religious fervour there was a growing party in all Churches which sought to make the evangelical scheme more attractive and practicable by accommodating it to the teachings of reason or common sense. This movement began with Socinianism, it was continued by Arminianism, and in the eighteenth century it was a great power in Germany as Rationalism, in England as Latitudinarianism, and in Scotland as Moderatism. The Lutheran Church was dominated for a time by a theological school which in the name of enlightenment even challenged the material principle of the Reformation. 'I am justified,' said a leading theologian on his death-bed, 'because it has ever been my purpose to be good and to do good.'[1] The scheme was further reconciled with the wisdom of this world by identifying the operations of the Holy Spirit with the influence of Christian teaching and example. In the Anglican and Presbyterian communions there was much preaching which left the impression that it is enough to fear God and try to do one's duty. Melanchthon had deplored in his day that there were famous Roman Catholic preachers who 'banished the gospel and instead of a sermon repeated the ethics of Aristotle,' and the poet Burns voiced the same charge of the Scottish evangelicals against the moderate ministers—

> The moral man they did define,
> But ne'er a word o' faith in't.

These experiments were followed by an evangelical revival on an international scale. In Germany the Lutheran Church as a whole was won back to loyalty

[1] Kahnis, *Dogmatik*, 1875, ii. p. 243.

to the gospel of the Reformation, and reverence for the distinctive evangelical experience. In England the Wesleyan mission stirred the indifferent masses and gathered many into a new communion, while an influential party within the national Church impressively preached the gospel of the grace of God as set forth in the Thirty-Nine Articles. The Church of Scotland, though it had been impoverished by evangelical secessions, became a chief instrument in a general awakening. New England, with its Puritan traditions and evangelists like Jonathan Edwards, was the scene of notable awakenings, while the evangelical message of the Methodists and Baptists met with a great response in the growing Commonwealth. Much was done to ensure that radical conversion was fortified by the due use of the appointed means of grace, and Methodism provided an edifying system of class-meetings under approved leaders. In the Calvinistic Churches congregational life was enriched by meetings for prayer and fellowship, by the enlistment of a large body of members in teaching and visitation, and by claiming the interest of the mass of the laity in missionary labours at home and abroad. And there were at least object-lessons as to what might be done to help those who desired to make it their chief end to be eminent Christians. The most notable was the example of German Pietists who organised agricultural communities, consisting largely of married persons, who gave to God and His cause the first place among their interests, and whose daily work was interwoven with devotional exercises and spiritual communion.[1]

---

[1] Spangenberg, *Constitution of the Unity of the Evangelical Brethren*, 1775.

We have noted in the first Protestant period a succession of religious movements, popularly known as Low, High and Broad Church, which were preceded and also followed by a revival of evangelical faith, sanctity and endeavour. And this sequence points to a general law which may be traced on a larger scale. The primitive Church was essentially evangelical, the Catholic Church became predominantly priestly and ritualistic, and when at the close of the Middle Ages it was much corrupted by the lusts of the flesh and invaded by humanism, there took place the outpouring of the Spirit that led to the Reformation. In this cycle the determining factors were the unsubdued forces of human nature that make for backsliding and apostasy, well-meant ecclesiastical efforts to check the downward trend, and another outpouring of the Spirit when there was reason to fear that the Church would be crushed or absorbed by the world. The policy of the Catholic Church, as was observed, was dictated by the conviction that it would make more of the obdurate human material if it learned from the Old Testament dispensation in which a priesthood ruled and the chosen people were placed under the yoke of a legal and sacrificial system. And the same motive goes far to explain the rise of a powerful High Church party in the Lutheran and Anglican communions. When it appeared that the unregenerate multitude with whose welfare a national Church was charged, ceased to be much attracted by preaching and was in danger of lapsing into utter irreligion, it was naturally sought to strengthen the hands of the ministry by making larger use of the moving appeal of 'the visible word' of the sacraments, and by sounding more confidently the note of authority to which human nature instinctively bows. There was also disappointment that so few of the class of the converted attained to a high plane of sainthood, and it was hoped that the aspiration would be fostered by bringing back the Catholic atmosphere. The leaders of the Broad Church party in the seventeenth and eighteenth centuries are to be honoured for their attempt to separate eternal verities from mere human opinions as well as from vain superstitions, and at a time when unbelief was coming in like a flood they did the service of witnessing to God and immortality, and insisting on duty as the indispensable form of the service of God. Moreover, they fostered in not a few souls the sense of deep spiritual needs that bespeaks a welcome for the gospel which promises peace of mind through friendship of God, and with it the power to live up to a high-pitched moral ideal. On the other hand, we may not belittle the results produced throughout the first Protestant period by the gospel-message that was enshrined in all the Confessions, proclaimed from the average pulpit, and exemplified in innumerable lives. Above all, the outstanding lesson of the period is that it began and ended with an evangelical revival. It was evangelical faith that brought into being the Protestant Churches in which a chastened High Church party and a moderate Broad Church party found a home and a sphere of usefulness; and it is unlikely that either of those or both together would have saved Protestantism from disintegration if its Churches had not possessed an evangelical core which, after a serious declension, was signally re-vivified and augmented by a fresh baptism with the Holy Ghost and with fire.

Chapter VI

PHILOSOPHICAL APPRAISEMENT

When philosophy resumed its labours in the modern world it was with the limitation, expressly accepted by Descartes and Locke, that in the sphere of divine things it might merely contribute to the statement and defence of articles of Natural Theology. It might not even discuss those cardinal Christian doctrines, derived from the special revelation, which, while not contrary to reason, were above reason, and only apprehended by faith. In this category were the doctrines of the Trinity, the Incarnation and the Atonement, and also the doctrine of regeneration by the Holy Spirit. It was not, however, to be expected that philosophy, which seeks to grasp things in their totality, could be permanently interdicted from pronouncing on the value of the knowledge which the ecclesiastical school of thought claimed to possess about the Supreme Being and the inner life of the Godhead. With the detachment of a Jewish philosopher Spinoza explored the Christian Holy of Holies, and found in it not the ineffable Three in One, but an impersonal Infinite that is the ground and soul of the universe; while in the next century a popular Rationalism rejected the mysteries of the faith, and reduced Christianity to the reasonable doctrines of God, the soul and immortality. To these succeeded the school of German idealists who emphatically held that all Christian dogmas fall to be judged by philosophy, but differed from the vulgar Rationalism in holding that Trinitarian and other dogmas contain a core of reliable and vital truths. They also took under their patronage the Christian doctrine of conversion practically ignored by Moral Philosophy, which offered as a poor substitute a programme of the formation of good character through the combination of instruction and discipline. It was a period that witnessed notable religious revivals, and the idealists even vied with pietists and Methodists in preaching the necessity of a conversion which involved a completely new attitude towards God, the world and man. On the other hand, the philosophical conception of conversion was a very radical modification of the doctrine which had been elaborated in Protestant theology, and which in the ministry to the multitude had been supported by the demonstration of the Spirit of power. The philosophical doctrine was, in fact, rather a reversion to one or other of the types of conversion previously described which had a vogue in ancient Greece and in the Hellenistic world. In the most recent period popular opinion became less and less sympathetic with the idea of the necessity of regeneration, and notable attempts were made from the philosophical side to rehabilitate, justify and glorify the natural man. In this chapter we shall review the types of conversion commended by Kant, Hegel and Schopenhauer, and thereafter examine the case for the natural man which was audaciously and brilliantly set forth by Friedrich Nietzsche.

The Protestant doctrine of conversion, which in the age of the Reformation was impressively commended by individual examples, became unpopular in the later seventeenth and in the eighteenth centuries when spiritual life became shallow and moral achievement very mediocre. Regeneration was felt to be far too big a word to describe the difference which their religion made in the vast majority of persons who professed the Christian faith and made use of the means of grace. The great Protestant Churches adhered formally to the teaching of their confessions on the subject, and there never failed a succession of evangelical preachers who called upon sinners to repent and believe the Gospel, but there was a growing section, known as liberal, moderate or latitudinarian, which minimised the idea of the new birth, and toned down the doctrinal presuppositions of human depravity and the work of the Holy Spirit.

The doctrine of conversion was modified in important particulars by the Socinian and Arminian sects, and it was completely emasculated in the school of the English Deists who accepted nothing that had an element of mystery, and was felt to be repugnant to common sense. For more than a generation the Lutheran Church was dominated by a rationalistic school which replaced the ideal of conversion by that of the formation through Christian influences of a respectable type of religious and moral character. For this purpose supernatural gifts of grace were held to be unnecessary in view of the natural God-given endowment of reason and conscience, and belief in supernatural help was even pronounced harmful as tending to make men relax their efforts to overcome their faults and to grow in piety and virtue.[1]

I

Although philosophy has long ceased to be the handmaid of theology, from time to time it has rendered it the service of calling attention to treasures in its keeping whose value it under-estimated, and of which it ought to make fuller use. This was done by Kant when the popular theology of his day set little store on, and even apologised for, the Catholic dogmas. In particular he reproached the so-called vulgar Rationalism with failing to appreciate the depth of the Christian doctrine of regeneration, and in the name of reason he reaffirmed the need of such a change, and the possibility of its accomplishment.[2]

In agreement with the Christian doctrine of original sin, and in opposition to optimistic estimates of human nobility, Kant held that the spiritual man as man is radically evil. What is wrong is that, though he acknowledges the obligation to obey the moral law, the maxim or principle on which he habitually acts is that he is entitled to violate the law when it runs counter to the promptings of self-love.[3] This holds of the species, even of the best of its members, and so overwhelming are the evidences of the depravity of human beings, civilised as well as savage, that we

---

[1] For the classic text-book of this school see Wegscheider, *Institutiones Theologicae Dogmaticae*.
[2] *Die Religion innerhalb der Grenzen der blossen Vernunft*, 1922, xlv. 47.
[3] *Ibid.*, p. 48.

do well, if we would not become misanthropes, to turn away our eyes from the sorry spectacle. So deeply rooted in human nature is this disposition to give the second place to the moral law and the first to self-love, that it must be regarded as innate. It is therefore necessary that man as man should be radically transformed. It is not enough to overcome particular failings and vices, and to leave the root of the evil untouched. What is needed is, not piece-meal reformation with minor amendments of character and conduct, but an alteration of the basis of character and of the habitual way in which the mind works.[1] Such a radical change may be thought as impossible as that a crooked beam should make itself straight, but we have the strongest grounds for believing in the possibility. The moral law commands us to become better men, and the thought necessarily implies that we can.[2] The sense of obligation to the moral law is implanted in human nature, and we have a haunting suspicion amounting to a conviction that we are unworthy to exist if we prefer pleasure or any such lower good to the dictates of the majestic law which issues through reason its imperious commands. And reverence for this law can so grow upon us as to raise the feelings to the pitch of enthusiasm when we are disposed to make the greatest sacrifices apart from any threat of punishment or promise of reward. Moreover, we may have faith that if we do our utmost to live up to the moral ideal our efforts will be seconded from

[1] *Die Religion innerhalb der Grenzen der blossen Vernunft*, xlv. 48.
[2] *Ibid.*, p. 55.

a higher source. The commands of the moral law continue to sing in our ears, and even if what we are able to do is insufficient, we have at least the ability to make ourselves receptive for help from an inscrutable power.[1] One fatal heresy is that God can give no salvation without making us good, another that He can make us good without our doing more than ask it in prayer, but the truth is that we must do all in our power to become good, when we may hope that what is beyond our power will be accomplished in co-operation with power from on high. It is added that on this point there has been much unnecessary and unprofitable controversy, for ' it is not needful to know what God does or has done for our salvation. Enough that we know what we have to do in order to deserve the divine help.' [2]

While Kant has the credit of reaffirming the necessity of conversion, and of leaving room in his scheme for a certain work of grace, his own doctrine must be thought an impoverishment of the evangelical scheme, and on the whole a reversion to a one-sided pre-Christian type. It was akin to the Stoic conception in that he attached chief importance to the ethical content of the character of the new man, and that, for the power needed to work the change, he chiefly looked to a natural response from the divine side of human nature to the demands of the majestic and imperious moral law. Still closer, perhaps, was the affinity of his regenerate man with the type of the Old Testament prophets of God in whose bones

[1] *Die Religion innerhalb der Grenzen der blossen Vernunft*, xlv. 48.
[2] *Ibid.*, p. 57.

the word of God burned as a fire, and of the psalmists
who loved His law, and found strength by meditating
on it day and night. He might, however, have learned
from the Old Testament experience that it was only a
select few who were changed through the impression
made on them by the sublimity of the moral law, and
that the commoner result is, as St. Paul said, that
instead of quickening and energising, it depresses and
provokes to rebellion. Moreover, in the case of Old
Testament converts the reverential loyalty was evoked
less by the law as such, than by the living God whose
holy will was expressed in it, and who supported it
by the sanctions of His almighty power. It may
also be thought that the prophets showed more
insight than the philosopher when they came to the
conclusion that the only way of effecting conversions
on a large scale was that God Himself should inter-
vene and pour out His Spirit without measure.
Kant's recognition of gracious aid in the struggle
was grudging, and he was not far from the Pelagian
doctrine, condemned by the Church as dishonouring
to God and harmful to man, according to which
man has to take the initiative and rely on his natural
God-given powers in the saving of his soul. He also
discarded two elements that supplied much of the
power of the message at the Reformation and in the
Puritan period. One was the doctrine that it was
the perfect sacrifice of the divine Son which made it
possible for God to forgive the sins of the penitent,
and to bestow upon him the Holy Spirit; and in
Kant's gospel the great sacrifice was little more than
a parable enshrining the truth that true spiritual

life includes the death of the natural man, and a resurrection to the dignity and calling of the new creature. Another element of the evangelical message that was discarded was the terror of the Lord which had been powerfully used to persuade men; and it is still a question whether, when the crude and material conceptions of Hell are dropped, there is not a duty of proclaiming in a better form the most certain and salutary truth that whatsoever a man soweth that shall he also reap, and that the wages of sin is death. And not the least defect of Kant's gospel was that he only called upon God at a late stage of the experience as the power that might give some aid in the ethical process, and that could be trusted to guarantee the eventual realisation of the chief good which blends blessedness with moral perfection. It may well be held that this was anything but an improvement on the evangel, which makes conversion to begin with the attainment of filial relations with God and to be confirmed and perfected in reliance on His continued gifts of grace.

II

The necessity of regeneration was the core of the Hegelian teaching in regard to the duty and the destiny of man, and there was a sense in which it was also affirmed of the Infinite Spirit that is the ultimate reality. 'If we should seek to gather up the Hegelian philosophy in a sentence,' wrote Edward Caird, 'it would be this—that the words "die to live" express not only the dialectic of

morals, but the universal principle of philosophy.' [1]
Self-renunciation as the way to self-realisation is the
leading idea which shines as a star through the
darkness of *Die Phänomenologie des Geistes*, and the
disciple furnishes a welcome exposition.

Taken in its application to morals, the maxim "die to live"
might be supposed to mean only that this world must be
sacrificed in order that the next may be won. The true
interpretation of the maxim is that the individual must die
to an isolated life—*i.e.* a life for and in himself, a life in which
the immediate satisfaction of desire as his desire is an end in
itself—in order that he may live the spiritual life, the universal life which really belongs to him as a spiritual or self-
conscious being. Now it is a simple psychological fact that
as we cannot know ourselves except in relation to objects
from which we distinguish ourselves, so we cannot seek our
own pleasure except in objects which are distinguishable
from that pleasure and which we desire for themselves. As
it is a condition of our intellectual life that we exist for
ourselves only as other things and beings exist for us, so it is
a condition of our practical life that we can realise ourselves
or live for ourselves only as we live for other ends and beings
than ourselves. Thus it appears that there is an element of
self-negation even in our most immediate theoretical and
practical existence, and that we must die to live—go out of
ourselves to be ourselves—even in the most sensuous and
selfish life we can possibly live. Obviously, however, this
does not take away the significance of the moral law, but
rather for the first time shows the possibility of obeying it,
as a law which is grounded in the real nature of man: a
law under which we not only *ought* to live, but under which
we *must* in some manner live if as rational beings we are to
live at all. We are thus also enabled to remove a mis-
conception which in many minds stands in the way of
acceptance of the principle of self-sacrifice as if it involved
a mere ascetic self-annihilation or a rejection of all the
positive elements of life. When it is seen that all that is

[1] *Hegel*, p. 44.

really positive in our life has a negative element in it, and that it is only through such negation of self that any positive good can ever be attained, it can no longer be apprehended that the *further* development of this negative or self-renouncing aspect of morality will impoverish human life, or strip it of any of its real sources of joy. The wider and completer is the good which we seek, *i.e.* the realisation of ourselves, the deeper and more thorough must be the negation of self on which it is based. More life and fuller, *that* we want; but, by a law that cannot be defeated or cheated, this fuller life is possible to us only through our sacrifice, renunciation or death of the immediate or natural self—the self which is opposed to the not-self, and which seeks a good for itself which is not a good for others. For it is only in breaking down the boundary that separates our life from the life of others that we can at the same time break down the boundary which prevents their life from becoming ours. St. Paul's saying, 'All things are yours, for ye are God's,' expresses the true conditions on which alone the limits of the individual life can be removed—viz. that it should cease to will itself except through the whole of which it is a part. The principle that he who loses his life in this sense saves it has another application. It forbids us to think of the universe, which is the manifestation of intelligence, and essentially spiritual, as a sphere in which all that we call higher interests are sacrificed to an adverse or indifferent fate. The moral principle that we must lose our lives in order to save them has therefore its counterpart and complement in a law of the universe according to which all the evils and sorrows that belong to the spiritual life (and in a world which is in its essence spiritual this ultimately means all evils and sorrows whatever) contain in them the 'promise and potency of a good in which they are not merely compensated, but taken up and transcended.' [1]

The idea of regeneration as thus expounded was commended by Hegel as the final and perfect idea reached in the process of thought which had

[1] Caird, *op. cit.*, pp. 212 ff. (condensed). Quoted by kind permission of the publishers, Messrs. Blackwood and Sons, Ltd.

long sought to establish right relations between the self on the one hand and God and the world on the other. The stages, as in other movements of the spirit, were the thesis, the antithesis and the higher synthesis. At the first stage the self was both worldly-minded and religiously-minded without being conscious of the conflict of the claims of the world and God. At the second stage there was a growing consciousness that a choice had to be made, the alternatives being to seek to possess the world and ignore God, or the ascetic way of seeking to possess God and despising and renouncing the world. At the crowning stage, attained in Christianity as rightly understood, was the assurance that the self possesses God as necessary for the development of its powers, and for the extension and deepening of its life. In his earlier writings Hegel saw in Christianity the representative of ascetic detachment from the world, but his mature opinion was that its attitude to the world was correctly divined by the Reformers who opposed to the ascetic ideal the saying of the apostle concerning those who are Christ's—'all things are yours.'

On the other hand, he departed considerably from the Christian conception of the content of the character and the experience of the regenerate man, and that both on the religious and the ethical side. In the matter of piety he gave the same central place as in Christianity to union with God, of whom it was declared that He is a Spirit, and as such essentially rational and moral; but the loving and trustful communion with Him, which was enjoyed by the

Christian, was gravely imperilled by the fact that it was left doubtful whether the absolute Spirit actually is a personal God who loves and cares for the individual soul, and whether even a consciousness can be attributed to Him other than that which has developed in the creatures which owe to him existence, preservation and enlightenment. Also there is a wide difference—not obviously in favour of the philosophical conception—between the Hegelian experience of realising a Kinship with God, approaching to identity, and the Christian experience of the pardoned sinner impelled by gratitude for undeserved mercy to make due return to his benefactor, and equipped for his tasks, as for his trials, by supplies of supernatural grace. On the ethical side the regenerate man of the Hegelian type was pledged to morality as of the essence of the absolute Spirit in which his higher life was rooted, and continuance in self-renunciation was dictated by the wisdom which knows it to be the only means to the sovereign good of self-realisation. But there are at least two points at which Hegel as moralist offends the Christian conscience, and it may well be thought that the superiority rests with the Christian ideal. The second great commandment, Jesus said, is, 'Thou shalt love thy neighbour as thyself,' and Hegel set himself to belittle it. 'Active love,' he says, 'for passive love has no meaning—aims at delivering another from evil, and conferring benefits upon him. And we must act on knowledge of what is good for him and bad for him, in short we must love him intelligently, otherwise our love may injure him even more than our hatred. The most beneficent and the richest of intelligent love is the activity of the State: so important is it, in fact, that beneficent individual action is comparatively insignificant and scarcely worth mentioning, and when coming into conflict with it is properly prohibited.'[1] No doubt Hegel rendered a real service by emphasising that the chief form in which the ordinary citizen obeys the command to love his neighbour as himself is by diligence and efficiency in his vocation, and by admonishing the State that its chief end is to promote the well-being of a people as a whole, with special attention to their spiritual well-being. But however much he may magnify the function of the State, and the ethical importance of the citizen's vocation, it must be evident that there remains, and will remain, a vast field from which the call comes to the individual to make a spontaneous and independent contribution to the guidance of the ignorant, the help of the weak, and the relief of the suffering.

The second serious declension from the Christian ideal was that for Hegel the truly great man is emancipated from the moral law. He becomes ecstatic, not about Jesus and the greatest of His disciples, but about Alexander the Great, Julius Caesar and Napoleon, and speaks most respectfully even of Caesar Borgia. 'World-historical men,' he says, 'the heroes of an epoch, were its clear-sighted ones; their deeds, their words, were the best of that time. This way of considering them excludes the view, due to envy, which makes them appear on

[1] *Phänomenologie des Geistes*, 1909, p. 317.

account of their passions not to have been moral
men. Every pedagogue has demonstrated that
Alexander and Caesar were immoral—for the same
poor reason that no valet sees a hero in his master.
The great men were not so unwise as to indulge a
variety of wishes and distract their attention from
their one aim. So mighty figures must necessarily
tramp down many an innocent flower, and break
in pieces every object that crosses their path.' [1]
To this conception of these historic figures as the
darlings of the world-spirit one may reasonably
prefer the view of the Old Testament prophets, that
God permitted while condemning their wickedness,
and over-ruled them for the advancement of His
Kingdom of righteousness, peace and brotherhood.

The Hegelian doctrine of dying to live met with
a considerable response among the intellectuals of
Germany and Britain, who accepted it as the theory
of life that it is a man's duty and also his interest
to seek to live not for his particular interests but in
accordance with the monitions of the absolute Spirit
and with an eye to universal obligations. But it
cannot be said that the doctrine made any impression on the general mind except in that it recalled
the saying of Christ that a man must lose his life if
he would find it, and also the example by which it
was enforced. Nor did the Hegelian school command a moral dynamic comparable to that of the
message which convinced men of sin, made them
fear the wrath of God against the impenitent, invited
them to trust for Christ's sake in a reconciled Father

---

[1] *Philosophie der Geschichte*, 3rd ed., 1848, pp. 39 ff.

in Heaven, and claimed them thenceforward for the service of God and man as new creatures in Christ Jesus, furnished with an enduement of power from on high for the completion of victory over the world and all its evils.

III

One of the most fruitful principles of the Hegelian system was the formation of a general law according to which the line of progress in the development of ideas, whether political, aesthetic or religious, has been through the conflict of affirmation and negation towards a higher synthesis in which the elements of truth in the conflicting positions are happily combined. But there is also a law of reaction which has complicated the situation, and when the synthesis has been reached it has usually proved to be the starting-point of further dissension in which the one-sided views, instead of being dropped as discredited, have been revived and supported with fresh zeal and energy. It was therefore not to be expected that the Hegelian doctrine of self-realisation through self-renunciation would finally settle the age-long conflict between the spiritual policies of self-affirmation and self-abnegation. Schopenhauer, the last Titanic figure of the idealistic school, revived the gospel of deliverance through flight from the world which had been pronounced to be the vital defect of Buddhism and of the ascetic type of Christian thought. To this there was an antithesis in the much more widespread and influential movement, most bravely and brilliantly represented by Nietzsche, who maintained that the natural man, so far being called to self-mortification, rather needs to become stronger, more efficient and more ruthless in the exercise of the will to power and the achievement of his self-gratifying aims.

Schopenhauer reached independently the same conclusions as Buddha: that the world is so full of misery it were better not to be; that no help may be looked for from God, who either does not exist, or does not exist for man; and that if man is to be delivered out of his miserable plight he needs to be radically changed in the spirit of his mind. 'Because we are what we should not be,' he says, 'we necessarily do what we should not do, and so there is necessary a complete transformation of our disposition and nature—a new birth issuing in a redemption.' [1] The radical evil of man's spiritual condition is that he is naturally dominated by the principle described as 'the will to live,' and makes it the end and aim of his being to preserve himself and to enrich himself, irrespective of the claims of others, with all of imagined good wherewith the world promises to make him happy. Listening to the voice of nature as it speaks through his own will one is given to believe—'I the individual am all in all, my preservation is the one important matter, nothing else is of any consequence.' From this foolish and fatal illusion we are delivered by Knowledge, and this is obtained along two lines. One is to listen to a second voice of nature heard in the external world, which humbles our pride by making an utter mock of the pretensions of the

[1] *Welt als Wille und Vorstellung*, 1919, ii. p. 693.

individual. 'Every day,' it says, 'I destroy millions of individuals as my sport and pastime, leaving them at the mercy of chance, the most capricious of my children, who hunts them down at his pleasure; and every day I create more and more millions.'[1] When we confine our attention to human experience we realise the essential stupidity of selfishness, as there is abundant evidence that the goods for which we earnestly strive yield far less pleasure than we anticipated, and that any indulgence we can hope to grant to our cravings only whets an insatiable appetite. 'Life,' it is observed, 'is a continuous deception alike in things great and small; we see paradises in the distance which on a nearer approach prove to be optical illusions; happiness ever lies in the past and the future, never in the present.'[2]

The suppression of will to life, with all that this involves of self-seeking, is normally carried out at three stages. A beginning is made when the self accepts the restrictions that are imposed by the moral law. Morality is a guiding light in the journey towards the goal of self-abnegation. In particular, the practice of justice and benevolence is a symptom that an effective start has been made in the process of unselfing, for he who has a conscience which he obeys is like a bird flapping its wings preparatory to a flight. It is, moreover, a law of spiritual culture that the performance of good deeds confirms and strengthens virtuous dispositions. In acting justly we not only refrain from injuring others but benefit ourselves by strengthening the spirit of

---

[1] *Welt als Wille und Vorstellung*, 1919, ii. p. 689.   [2] *Ibid.*, p. 657.

self-denial. Charity in its biblical sense is still more
salutary, as it impels us at real cost to ourselves to
help others to bear particular burdens, with the
result that we come to live in a real sense outside of
ourselves, and self-renunciation becomes a spiritual
habitude. The second stage is that we begin to be
perfected through suffering. He who has realised
that the world does not exist to provide him with
happiness will profit by and even come to welcome
suffering, knowing that 'it is the means by which one
is recalled from the wrong road to self-affirmation,
and set in the right road of self-renunciation.' [1]
Though life proves to be anything but pleasurable,
he has at least the satisfaction of finding that things
fall out in accordance with his insight into the world-
order and his modest expectations. Above all, he
knows that suffering is for the good of his soul, and
endures like the invalid undergoing a treatment
whose pains he interprets as evidence that he is on
the way to sound and lasting health. The beneficent
discipline is crowned by the painful experiences and
the gloomy prospects of old age. It is true that all
do not profit by the last means of grace, for there
are many old men in whom the worship of self per-
sists in the miserable forms of avarice and vanity, but
it is at least well calculated to promote sanctification
through the knowledge that the powers are surely
decaying, and that death, the irresistible spoiler and
destroyer, stands at the door. 'Death' is thus discovered to be the true purpose of life. 'It is the
result and the résumé of life,' it is said, 'gathering

---

[1] *Welt als Wille und Vorstellung*, 1919, ii. p. 721.

up the moral which was taught bit by bit throughout its course—viz. that the whole of the striving was vain and inconsistent, and that escape from it is nothing less than a redemption.' [1] So great indeed is our debt to the destroyer whose approach humbles our pride, and shatters our selfish plans, that the agnostic pessimist approves of the prayer commended by the Church that we be delivered from sudden death. And this consideration supplies a good answer to the taunt that if the pessimist really believes what he teaches he should hasten to commit suicide. He may cherish the hope that, when mankind is fully enlightened, arrangements will be made with general consent for a radical solution of the problem by racial suicide, but it would be arguable that in existing conditions the individual should live as long as possible in order to profit to the full by the unselfing discipline of this painful earthly life, while pending any general resolution of suicide. Charity suggests that the individual should complete his allotted span because of its opportunities of bringing light and comfort to his fellow-sufferers.

The pessimism which is the pre-supposition of Schopenhauer's gospel cannot rank higher than a possible opinion based on an arbitrary selection from the facts of experience. Human life is full of suffering, but to call it martyrdom is a gross exaggeration, for, apart from the assurance of their instincts that it is supremely worth preserving, ordinary people find it good because of the interest of their occupations, their homes and their recreations, while

[1] *Welt als Wille und Vorstellung*, 1919, ii. p. 732.

familiarity and hope combine to make it tolerable even under the most dismal conditions. Besides, even if there were a demonstrable balance of misery, it would not follow that life is not worth having, for one may well think it better than the condition of a clod of earth, that he awoke out of unconsciousness and embarked on a thrilling venture into an unknown world and an unknown future, and above all that he was given the opportunity of rising above the plane of the animal to the dignity of a rational, moral and spiritual being claiming kinship with the Highest. Moreover, it was only by taking a very one-sided view of existence that colour was given to the theory that the active principle manifest in the order of things is of the nature of a ruthless demoniac force. If it be true that it has made the world a scene of incessant strife and suffering, it is equally obvious that our race owes to it, not only the marvellous constructive and aesthetic creations of the universe in which it has found a home, but also the gift of the intellect that produced science and philosophy, of the genius that added to knowledge the beauties of literature and art, and of the con-science which subjects to the jurisdiction of the moral law the gratification of animal lusts and the further-ance of selfish interests. It should also have been observed that while in the physical world it would seem that nature builds up to the end that it may forthwith proceed to disintegrate and destroy, in the realm of life and spirit, as pointed out by writers like Bergson following St. Paul, there is abundant evid-ence that the governing power works for the conservation and the perfecting of the value which it has brought into existence.

Schopenhauer's scheme of conversion, rooted as it was in pessimism and agnosticism, embodied a conception of the character of the new man which must be held to be a grievous impoverishment of the Christian conception. He gave powerful support to the Christian criticism of the natural man, but he did not replace him by the design of a new creature embodying all the higher potencies of the human spirit. While retaining the cardinal virtues of the ethical tradition, with the Christian addition of charity, he ruled out the graces of faith and hope which spring up in communion with God, and, from the aesthetic no less than from the religious point of view, it may well be held that the soul has a greater dignity and wealth of life when in addition to its human relationships it is knit by ties of love, trust and loyalty to a God who unites with the power of the Creator the grace of the Redeemer. It was also a culpable emasculation of the idea of the new man to prescribe to him the spirit of defeatism in relation to the world in preference to the virile Christian spirit most clearly voiced in Protestantism which accepts as obligatory the tasks that are set man in the providential order, and purposes not to flee from the world, but to overcome and possess the world through union with God and in the service of God.

In regard to the second vital matter—the means of conversion — Schopenhauer's scheme was conspicuously lacking in power. As with Buddha, his chief means of persuasion was to make men feel disgust at the conditions of the human lot, and fear of the consequences unless there be a change of heart; but the German philosopher was at a disadvantage as compared with the Indian sage in that he could not assume belief in future punishment in the form of an endless series of rebirths, with the result that his scheme was limited to the formation of a temporary school of disciples which could not even be consolidated into a monastic order. The most radical defect of his system, however, was that, while undertaking in the transformation of the natural man the most difficult of all tasks, he essayed it in contempt and defiance of the European experience of the Christian centuries, which has been to the effect that the renovation of man can be and has been brought about in a deep and rich sense, when sought in reliance upon the Creator who impressed His image on man.

IV

A marked feature of the latest period of human history was the resuscitation of the spirit of the natural man, and the attempt to justify his self-regarding aims. An age of unexampled material progress offered to individuals unusual opportunities of rising to wealth, power and honour, and the competitor was confirmed in the disposition to secure for himself the largest possible share of worldly treasures by the assurance that by doing the best for himself, especially by success in business, he would most effectually promote the general well-being. Still more nakedly was selfishness revealed in the col-

lective personality of nations which in recent times,
and partly because of the self-consciousness stimulated
by popular education, have had a fresh access of the
spirit of self-glorification and self-aggrandisement.
The case for the natural man has also been pleaded
by powerful apologists, while the Christian ideal, of
which the worst said by former critics was that it
was impracticable, has been pronounced to be not
even deserving of respect. In the Continental movement the teaching of Nietzsche has been one of the
chief intellectual factors, and it is profitable to consider his indictment of the Christian character, and
his conception of the higher pattern of humanity by
which it is to be replaced.

The Christian conception of the new man, with
the graces of sympathy and non-resistance, was traced
to its origin in the mentality of the slave. 'It was
the Jews,' he says, 'a people born to slavery, as
Tacitus and the whole world said, who wrought the
miracle of a reversal of values, thanks to which
during twenty centuries life acquired a new and
dangerous spice in that it identified the rich with
the wicked, and made of "the world" a term of
reproach. What gave the Jews their importance
is that they were the ringleaders in the revolt of
the slaves.' [1] 'And it was the spirit of the slave that
became the genius of Christianity, the religion which
serves and flatters the aspirations of the common
herd.' [2] In it we discover the influence of his
characteristic traits, his inability to appreciate the

---

[1] *Jenseits von Gut und Böse : Werke*, 1903, vii. p. 127.
[2] *Ibid.*, p. 136.

virtues of his superiors, his distrust of their standards, his high regard for all that goes to spare or relieve suffering—gentleness, meekness, the warm heart, the helping hand. It also reflects the slave's fear of his master, and his resentment at the loss of his liberty, and menaces with punishment all that is powerful and dangerous to the general mass of mankind. Thus lacking in dignity, the Christian rule of life is further declared to be detrimental to the best interests of the species.

'Injure no man, help all to the utmost of thy power' is a maxim which not only offends every man of good taste, but which is dishonest and harmful in a world whose essence and value is the will to power.[1] It is granted that faith in God as the Supreme Ruler once had its uses, for the most needful thing for the ordinary man and for the herd is to have a master train them to obedience, but the throne of the divine governor was now vacant, and the superior man, with no God to look to but himself, would rise to new heights.[2]

In place of the Christian ideal, discounted as servile or plebeian, Nietzsche proposed the aristocratic ideal, adumbrated, though imperfectly realised, by the upper class of the progressive peoples of ancient and modern times. The ruling caste had its distinctive type of morality, and though it has been temporarily eclipsed, it will again be reaffirmed and strengthened with general approval. In this aristocratic type of morality, good is the equivalent of

---

[1] *Jenseits von Gut und Böse : Werke*, 1903, vii. p. 115.
[2] *Also sprach Zarathustra*, vi. p. 418.

noble, bad of contemptible. The objects of contempt are the coward, the anxious, the small-minded, he who is bent on narrow utilities or small gains, he who is habitually suspicious, he who doglike prostrates himself and lets himself be kicked, the begging sycophant, and above all the liar. The true man succours those in distress, and is open-handed, but less from sympathy than from an impulse to bestow out of his fulness of life and excess of power. At all events, he never dreams of giving to sympathy, service of others, disinterest, the central place in his moral scheme. Rather is an essential feature contempt and suspicion of the warm heart. The mark of the noble soul is its reverence for itself, and respect for those —and only for those—who share its dignity and its virtues. He honours in himself the man of power, which includes power over himself; he can speak and be silent, and be strict and hard towards himself.

'Egotism,' we read, 'is of the essence of the noble soul—the unshakable faith that to a being such as we are, other beings must be naturally subject and sacrifice themselves to him. The noble soul adopts this actual attitude of its egoism without any mark of interrogation, without any feeling of harshness, compulsion, caprice—rather as something which must be rooted in a primeval law of things; if it looked for a name for it, it would say—it is justice. It grants that there are others of like rank—for there is a celestial mechanism understood by all stars. It honours itself in them and in their rights. Retribution is banal. Among equals grace has no meaning, and in fact an evil odour. It does not like to look up—it looks

K

either before it—horizontally and slowly, or down—
it knows itself to be a life.' [1]

What gives Nietzsche's message an extraordinary
interest is that he was the prophet and apologist of
latter-day movements which have stirred nations to
their depths and reorganised their activities, and
which are regarded by one half of those concerned
with admiration and hope, by the other with detestation and fear. For their salvation he longed for the
appearance of leaders with the will to power as their
ruling impulse, after the type of the blond beast that
works its will in the jungle—whose conscience will be
steeled, and their heart changed to bronze so that they
can calmly bear the weight of their heavy responsibility.
For them God is dead, but they may be thought to
be the spirit of a powerful, crafty ironical demon—
figured of old as Dionysus who has a liking for the
race, and whose wish is that they may become
stronger, more wicked and more profound.[2] 'What
a boon would it be, what a deliverance from an
oppression that is growing intolerable would be the
advent of absolute rulers of the European herds.' [3]
With this dream of the strong man and of like-
minded instruments went an overweening contempt
for the common herd and its garrulous and quarrel-
some representatives, and also fierce hostility to the
Jews, who besides plundering the civilised world had
foisted on it as ideals the aspirations of the slave and
the weakling. The many would be put in their
proper place, and an end made of the preposterous

---

[1] *Jenseits von Gut und Böse: Werke*, 1903, vii. p. 251.
[2] *Ibid.*, p. 272.   [3] *Ibid.*, p. 130.

idea that their creatures should be put in charge of
the destinies of nations. A governing principle of
the needed leaders was that the great end justifies
all needed means, and in particular war was glorified
as the chiefest means of putting the world right, and
maintaining its virility.

'My brothers in war,' says Zarathustra, 'I love you
from the bottom of my heart. I know the hatred and
envy of your heart. You are not great enough not
to know hatred and envy. But you should be great
enough not to be ashamed of it. You ought to be
ever looking for an enemy, for your enemy—and
some of you hate at the first glance. Seek your
enemy. Love peace as the means to new wars, and
the shorter the peace the better. I call you not to
work but to battle, not to peace but to victory.
A man can only be silent and sit quiet when he has
bow and arrows; otherwise he gabbles and quarrels.
They say a good cause sanctifies war, I say a good
war sanctifies every cause. War and courage have
done greater things than sympathy. It was not your
compassion but your courage that rescued the miserable. They call you heartless, but your heart is
genuine; you are ugly, well then, wrap yourself in
the sublime mantle of your ugliness. Revolt is the
nobility of the slave; let your nobility be obedience,
let your orders be acts of obedience.' [1]

On the other hand, Nietzsche seemed to differ
widely from latter-day dictators in his conception of
the State. He calls it the new idol, and the most
cold-blooded of all monsters. Its blackest lie is—

---

[1] *Also sprach Zarathustra*, vi. pp. 66 ff.

'I, the State, am the people.' As a fact, those who made the peoples were creators who generated life, and the modern worshippers of the State are destroyers who set death-traps for a people. The difference between people and State appears from the fact that a people hates the State as a sinner against its customs and rights. The State is a liar, all that it possesses it has stolen, and it has confused the ideas of good and evil. The monster growls 'I am the finger of God,' and those with long ears and short sight fall on their knees before it. Where the State ends begin the rainbow and the bridges of the super-man.[1] It is, however, to be observed that the State against which Nietzsche inveighed as a stupid and baleful monster was only one form of it—the democratic State, governed by talkers who should themselves be slaves, and whose policy is to assert the supposed rights, and relieve the distresses of the common herd. Some form of State is necessary, and his strictures do not apply to a State constituted by a superman organising it according to his good pleasure, and who in doing so acts like the aristocrat who, while despising them, does the part of a good shepherd by the herd. It is, all the same, a substantial point of difference that, while latter-day dictators desire that the herd should multiply indefinitely, Nietzsche held that it was already far too numerous, and that nothing was more desirable than the elimination of the vast body of the inferior and superfluous.

Nietzsche has been described by an admirer of his genius as 'a neurotic professor who would fain have

[1] *Also sprach Zarathustra*, vi. pp. 69 ff. (condensed).

been an unbridled tyrant.' [1]   He had two souls—
one inspired by Apollo, which found its chief end in
Science and Art, the other inspired by Dionysus
which yearned to realise itself in passionate and
heroic action; and there were moods in which he
felt the *saeva indignatio* of the prisoner and vented it
upon the order of things and on himself as one of
its victims. His honesty was equal to his genius, and
honour must be paid him for his courage in declaring
the secrets of the heart of the natural man, and undertaking to defend him against the censures of religion
and morality. But his main theses have met with
their chief support from elemental instincts of human
nature, not from reason and conscience and the divine
stratum in which they are rooted. He scouted and
dismissed the Christian ideal as plebeian, and commended in its stead an ideal breathing the aristocratic
spirit; and while no doubt there is a mass of commonplace Christianity that is vulgar enough, he ought to
have observed that there is an affinity between the
truly aristocratic spirit and the spirit of Christ. It
was no accident that at the close of the Roman
period and in the Middle Ages many of the greatest
of the saints and founders of monastic orders were
attracted by the vision of a greater loyalty and a
higher chivalry than they found among their kindred
in the seats of the mighty, and had the conviction
that as soldiers of Christ they did not fall but rose
in the scale of dignity. It is also noteworthy that
Napoleon, his supreme example of the higher type
of man that is to be, bowed in reverence before

---

[1] Windelband, *Geschichte der Philosophie*, 1921, ii. p. 566.

Christ as the leader, more than man, whose Kingdom will have no end. But the chiefest vice of the system was the conception that the mark of a higher humanity is to assert a self-seeking ideal, and it was an insult to the race to suppose that, having worshipped the loving and self-sacrificing Christ as God manifest in the flesh, it will come to see the highest in the blond beast of the jungle.

CHAPTER VII

THE SCIENTIFIC INVESTIGATION

I

In recent times the theological treatment of conversion has been supplemented by research professedly conducted on the lines and within the limited range of Natural Science. 'Our attempt,' wrote a pioneer, 'shall be to get at the moral and spiritual processes at work during conversion, rather than to establish any doctrine. We have before us a purely inductive investigation, to take the bare records of this class of experiences without anything to be proved or to guide us except the axioms of scientific criticism, and to view them in the light of scientific psychology.' [1] In practice the psychologists concerned have seldom confined themselves to observing, classifying and explaining the phenomena, but have made some assessment of the value of the spiritual experiences. And value-judgments are imperative for the applied sciences in which the results of psychological research are utilised for the benefit of society. The art of education presupposes a standard of intellectual and moral excellence to which a human being ought to aspire, and it behoves the educationalist to have a conviction as to whether religion has a place in the

[1] Starbuck, *The Psychology of Religion*, 1899, p. 21.

scheme, and if so, how it is best fostered. As a fact, the leading authorities in this field have favoured the inculcation of religious principles by teaching and practice, though none of note have urged that it should be a chief aim of a school to effect in the pupils a conversion of the type commended by the evangelical tradition. The interest of the medical profession has been bespoken for conversion by the fact that in its most pronounced form it involves an experience of inward upheaval and distress which may be followed by an access of peace and energy, but may also issue in a persisting condition of melancholy and enfeeblement. Psychiatrists have differed widely in their valuation of the intense religious experiences from the point of view of health, and while one school has welcomed the service to humanity of the Christian Gospel, another has rudely challenged the Christian estimate of the salutariness of the grief of the penitent, and the dignity of the saint and the mystic. Nor has the limitation of the inquiry to the empirical sphere been observed by all who claimed to be first and last the representatives of science. For scientists are also human beings with an impulsion to see things as a whole, and to divine the meaning and worth of man's existence; and while some have concluded that scientific explanation needs to be completed by the recognition of the powers of a higher spiritual world, there is a growing opinion that what has been learned about the operation of natural causes in this field is sufficient to make the theory of divine agency a groundless and gratuitous hypothesis.

II

OLD AND NEW METHODS

The Christian Church had previously done much work in the field now claimed for religious psychology, and largely by first-hand observation and with an interest in proximate causes. In a scientific investigation the primary aim is to get at the facts, and for this purpose the Church had the services of a great body of clergy that was in touch with most individuals and families professing the faith, and was taken so far into their confidence either by enforced or spontaneous confession. Examples of the greatest results achieved were recorded in the biographies of notable converts and eminent saints, while the shortcomings were rebuked in pastoral letters weighty with the voice of authority, and by great preachers who brought the divine searchlight to bear upon the actual spiritual conditions. The Protestant Churches have produced an abundance of books and articles which throw light on the state of piety and morals among the people to whom they minister, and from the Foreign Mission field there has flowed a steady stream of reports revealing spiritual results which, while doubtless very mixed, are comparable at the best with the fruits of the apostolic mission to the Gentiles.[1] In the ecclesiastical inquest, moreover, much attention was given to the proximate causes of religious experience, since it is Christian doctrine that the renewal of souls is normally effected by the Holy

---

[1] Allier, *Psychologie de la Conversion chez les peuples non-civilisés.*

Spirit working through observable instruments. It was generally agreed that the chief means are the word, the sacraments and prayer, but it was matter of controversy whether the word or the sacrament is the principal means of grace. The survey was extended to the mental dispositions and the social factors that have a bearing on the spiritual life. Moreover, there were theologians, notable among them St. Augustine and Jonathan Edwards, who combined the interests and the capacity of a gifted psychologist with their zeal for the glory of God and for the salvation of souls. Nor may it be overlooked that the Church has systematically sought to make practical applications of its ever-growing knowledge of human nature, and of the instrumental causes operative in the spiritual sphere. Practical Theology includes Homiletics, which gives guidance to preachers in the persuasive presentation of the divine message both to the converted and the unconverted; Catechetics, which deals with the nurture and upbringing of spiritual minors; and Poimenics, which fully expounds the aims and the methods of a shepherd of the flock.

The service rendered by the American school of religious psychology was to make an intensive investigation of the phenomena in a selected group representative of the higher reaches of spiritual life in a section of latter-day Protestantism. To this end Starbuck addressed a questionnaire to 192 persons who had been 'conscious of a real turning-point in the beginning of a new life,' and elicited their testimony as to the preparatory stage, the

essential nature and the fruits of the exceptional
experience. Recognising also that many become
good Christians as the result of growth, he addressed
to 232 persons of this class a set of questions as to
the special features of their spiritual history. The
same method was used by Stanley Hall, Leuba, Coe,
Pratt and others.[1] A generation later, Dr. Elmer T.
Clark similarly examined a larger company which included 985 Methodists, 366 Presbyterians, 252 Baptists
and 133 members of 'the Confirmation group of
Churches.'[2] The drawback was that these witnesses
were representatives of a religious period which, if
not decadent, is commonplace. William James found
much more valuable material in earlier confessions
and biographies of outstanding converts. The inquest
has been followed up on both sides of the Atlantic
by psychologists, historians and philosophers with a
growing preference for the literary sources.

III

The Empirical Facts

The general findings of the psychological school
were that Christianity continues to produce examples
of a radical transformation of character, but that
there is much greater variety than theology had
recognised, in the attainment, the forms and the
content of the experience.

That conversions still occur in which the centre of

---

[1] Leuba, *A Psychological Study of Religion.* Coe, *The Spiritual Life.*
Pratt, *The Psychology of Religious Belief.*
[2] *The Psychology of Religious Awakening,* 1929, p. 26.

gravity is completely changed is emphasised by most of the investigators. 'Conversion,' says Starbuck, 'is characterised by more or less sudden changes from evil to goodness, from sinfulness to righteousness, and from indifference to spiritual insight and activity.' [1] 'To be converted,' says James, 'to be regenerated, to receive grace, to experience religion, to gain assurance, are so many phrases which denote the process, gradual or sudden, by which a self hitherto divided, and consciously wrong, inferior, and unhappy, becomes unified and consciously right, superior, and happy, in consequence of its firmer hold upon religious realities.' [2] The essential notes of the experience, according to Coe, are that 'the subject's very self seems to be profoundly changed,' and 'the change includes a sense of attaining to a higher life, or to emancipation or enlargement of the self.' [3] An Italian scientist has criticised the American school, reduces conversion to a moral reformation, and declares that for the Catholic 'it is an exceptional process representing an intellectual and moral regeneration of the person in whom it occurs.' [4]

On the other hand, it has been made increasingly clear that in the spiritual realm, as in every other sphere of life, the unity consists with much variety. It was observed, to begin with, that there are marked differences in the time taken to effect the trans-

[1] *Op. cit.*, p. 21.
[2] *Varieties of Religious Experience*, 1903, p. 189. (Published by Messrs. Longmans, Green & Co., and quoted by kind permission of Mr. Henry James.)
[3] Coe, *The Psychology of Religion*, p. 153.
[4] De Sanctis, *Religious Conversion*, p. 40.

formation. The unquestionably regenerate fell into two divisions: those who had undergone a sudden conversion, and those who had reached the high spiritual plane by the way of gradual growth. Each of these divisions, moreover, showed a considerable variety of types and also of degrees of excellence in each type. Special attention was devoted to the class which witnessed to the cataclysmic conversion, and it was elicited that individual impressions differed widely on two important points: the nature of the blessings they had received in conversion, and the source to which they owed the deliverance. In reply to his question, 'In what did the change consist?' Starbuck reports that forgiveness was put in the first place by 16 per cent. of his witnesses, while 14 per cent. were chiefly conscious of attaining to 'oneness with God, friends, etc.' [1] What the other 70 per cent. deemed to be the central blessing was not brought out owing to the peculiar arrangement that the persons examined were classified as witnessing either to the benefits received or to the power which conveyed it, but might not appear in both classes. The normal accompaniment of conversion was described as an access of joy, peace and happiness, and it was the starting-point of a new life which had the general character of a process of unselfing. Of a group of 151 men examined, 43 mentioned as the chief result 'a closer relation to God,' 4 'a closer relation to Christ,' 34 'a closer relation to nature,' 42 'love for others,' 28 'desire to help others.' The testimony of 150 women was substantially the same. [2] The

---

[1] *Op. cit.*, Table XI. p. 94. [2] *Op cit.*, Table XVI. p. 128.

variety of types was most clearly disclosed by the answers to the question, 'Did the change come through or in spite of your own thought, deliberation and choice?' The largest group, given as 23 per cent., spoke of 'a spontaneous awakening in which the new life burst forth without any apparent immediate cause.' A second group, surprisingly given as only 10 per cent., took the further step of ascribing the deliverance to 'the special help and grace of God.' A third, given as 11 per cent., recalled the experience as one of self-surrender in which, after vain efforts to put themselves right with God, their pride was broken, and their cry was, 'Lord, I have done all I can, I leave the whole matter to Thee.' In contrast with these, a small class, given as 8 per cent., remembered as the decisive factor the determined exercise of will by which they yielded to God and dedicated their lives to Him.[1]

The experience in which the Christian character is gradually built up was similarly investigated, when the subjects were asked to 'mark out the stages of their growth,' and state 'what they felt now to be the trend of their life.' It was brought out that there is often a serious check and set-back to the happy development in the case of those who go on from a Christian home and the Sunday School to a liberal education, when they are assailed with doubts as to the authority of the Bible, the divinity of Christ and the existence of God. It was found, however, that few settled down in mere negations, but that

---

[1] *Op. cit.*, Table XI. p. 94.

most centred on a course of reconstruction which, though it left them with a liberal theology, at least meant the recovery of faith in God and Christ, and a sustained endeavour to live the Christian life. One of the queries was, 'What would you be and do if you realised your ideals?'—and practically all witnessed to an unselfing which gave them a Christian conception of their strict end. The distinction was that one group laid the emphasis on love and devotion toward God, another on altruistic service of their fellow-men.[1] Among those who gradually developed into good Christians there was a large class which had escaped the stage of serious stumbling and backsliding. And in this class two groups were distinguished. One was a select company 'whose religious life had flowed onward like a stream, enlarging and growing, but striking no obstructions and forming no cataracts.'[2] The other and larger company consisted of persons who, though spared the worst ordeal, had tended to coldness and stagnation, until they received a fresh emotional stimulus, whether from the services of the sanctuary or from a Christian friendship, that rekindled their love and revived their purpose of a new obedience.[3]

No great addition has been made by this investigation to the knowledge of the phenomena previously possessed by the Church. The principal generalisation is that there is a great variety of religious experience on the highest level, and if this was little recognised in Confessions of Faith and doctrinal systems, it has

[1] Op. cit., Table XVI. p. 128.
[2] Elton Clark, The Psychology of Religious Awakening, p. 45.
[3] Op. cit., pp. 42 ff.

ever been the working theory of the Christian ministry, with much support from the practice of our Lord Himself, that there is much diversity in the religious experience of the best, and that even its most rudimentary forms are to be judged with charity and optimism. That some become eminent Christians by the way of a gradual conversion, and more by the way of gradual growth, was axiomatic for the Catholic Church, and the great Protestant Churches soon realised, if they ever doubted, that it is by Christian nurture and training that the general body of those who shine as lights in the world is most surely recruited. The service of the American school at this point was to remind preachers and pastors that, if their task is the gradual remaking of the natural man, there is also need to work and pray that the process be completed and crowned in professing Christians by a radical transformation, and also to find opportunities of calling to repentance and faith the growing mass of professed and unprofessed unbelievers and worldlings. It may not, however, be said that the psychological examination threw much fresh light on the definite conversion that was specially studied. It was hailed by William James as a real advance in knowledge when Starbuck distinguished the volitional and the non-volitional types of conversion, but the patristic Church was well aware of the volitional type when it condemned the Pelagian school which maintained that the experience of salvation by self-effort was the authentic type, and when it supported the Augustinian school which attributed the initiative and the deliverance to the grace of God. It is to the credit of the psychologist that he detected two varieties of the non-volitional type, described as a spontaneous awakening and sense of the divine, and also an intermediate form described as self-surrender, all of which had previously passed without closer scrutiny as Augustinian. But it is puzzling that he found no representatives of the semi-Pelagian school, which ascribes conversion to co-operation between the returning sinner and a gracious God. It must be supposed that the failure to discover a semi-Pelagian group was due to a defect in the questionnaire, for the conception of conversion as the result of divine and human co-operation has always been widely held among the laity and has had much support from latter-day theologians.

IV

Causal Explanation

The truly novel contribution from the scientific side is the account given of the proximate causes of the exceptional spiritual experiences. Religious thinkers had been much interested in these causes, but in their treatment natural and supernatural factors were blended, while the psychologist may only take cognisance of forces belonging to the natural order. The conclusions reached implied that the Church has greatly exaggerated the work done in conversion by the so-called means of grace, and that the chief causes of conversion are to be found in active principles of human nature whose far-reaching influence theology had failed to detect.

L

1. According to the evangelical scheme, the principal means by which men are brought to repentance and faith in Christ is the word of God contained in the Scriptures. Augustine was converted by the text, 'Put ye on the Lord Jesus Christ'; Luther by the text, 'The just shall live by faith'; and Bunyan's pilgrim is introduced as reading the mighty book which moved him to cry, 'What must I do to be saved?' Holding this view, Protestant Churches have made the reading and preaching of the word the staple of religious services, while their Bible Societies have circulated the Scriptures by the million in more than a thousand languages. That they were mistaken seemed to be established when, of a group of persons questioned as to what produced their conversion, 19 per cent. ascribed it to social pressure, 13 per cent. to example, while only 10 per cent. attributed it to teaching, and not a single person to the reading of the Bible.[1] It is, however, probable that the queries were not sufficiently searching on this point, and that almost all would have agreed that what is best entitled to rank as the instrumental cause is the Gospel contained in the Scriptures which had been made known to them by preachers and teachers, commended by impressive examples of goodness, and endorsed by the sentiment of a religious community. In Clark's research more attention was paid to the power of ideas, and it was brought out that instruction in evangelical doctrine is the normal antecedent of the typical evangelical conversion.

[1] Elton Clark, *op. cit.*, p. 127.

2. The truly original and challenging contribution from the scientific side was that the theological account of the proximate causes of conversion was found quite inadequate, and the chief rôle was ascribed to principles of human nature which had not been suspected of a religious function.

(a) A general explanation of which much has been made is that the spiritual change is a by-product of adolescence. From Starbuck's tables it appeared that conversions begin with the approach of puberty, reach the peak between the ages of 16 and 17, decline steadily in the twenties, and rarely occur after the age of 40. Without doubt the great majority of those who have the definite experience are young persons, and it is obvious that youth disposes to higher ventures of the spirit. It is the stage at which the soul can become aflame with a passion for knowledge, the realm of the beautiful can claim a life for art or letters, and a call to self-sacrifice in a great cause can prevail over the attractions of pleasure and profit; and it is natural that at the same stage some should be deeply impressed by the sublimities of the spiritual world, and moved to dedicate themselves to the service of the Most High. But it is also on the threshold of his career that the natural man asserts himself with loud demands for the gratification of his passions, and it is probable that even in evangelical circles the proportion of young men definitely converted was less than that of the prodigals who brought sorrow and shame into Christian homes. It is therefore unwarrantable to specify as the cause proper of religious conversion a merely physical state.

(b) The observation that conversion is on the whole an adolescent phenomenon has suggested that the driving-power is derived from the sexual instinct. The thesis has been thus formulated: 'Literally we may say that God is love, sex-love sometimes in disguise and indistinctly recognised as such by the lover whose love-sick longings create a god to take the place of the undiscovered and much-craved human lover.'[1] Freud agrees that the instinct has suggested objects of religious faith and directed to them stores of energy, but for him the desire or libido includes the tender emotion and kindred sentiments by which lust has been overlaid and transcended in the human species. It must be admitted that the love wherewith human beings love God is the same affection with which a husband loves his wife and a wife her husband, and that there are those who, denied this happiness on earth, have been moved thereby to seek it in heavenly places. But there are other facts which are in conflict with the generalisation. There are many men and women who, though they have found happiness in wedded life, are drawn thereby not less but more to the love and service of the God whom they worship as the giver of all blessings that have enriched their lives.

(c) According to Adler, the source and power of religion is to be found in the instinct of which one of the names is self-assertion or positive self-feeling. Under the conditions of human life we are constantly

---

[1] Schroeder quoted by Thouless, *The Psychology of Religion*, 1924, p. 128.

being made to feel that we are weak and insignificant creatures, many have a habitual sense of inferiority, and there is an inward compulsion to find some way of viewing and interpreting our position that will restore our confidence in ourselves and make our circumstances seem more than tolerable. And the way taken in religion was to believe in a divine Being who treats us as His children and by whom we are protected and blessed.[1]

The power of the instincts is all-pervading, and it may be granted that they have made their influence felt at many points in the matter of the development and of the propagation of religion. It may indeed be said that religion could not have found a place in human life unless it had been able so far to come to an understanding with the instincts as to establish a *modus vivendi*, and procure a measure of co-operation. But the whole, or even the chief, explanation of religious experience can only be found on that plane by shutting our eyes to the higher side of experience, which includes the sense of duty and the vision of God. And it is on the higher, not on the lower, plane of human nature that the true cause of conversion is to be sought. 'The instincts had some part in it, but it is not merely a conflict of instincts. There is always some ideal involved, either in the form of an ideal person who claims us, or some ideal of character and service that we seek to attain. It may be a conflict of instinctive impulses with the ideal, but it is never merely a conflict of instincts. The realisation of an ideal cannot come wholly out

[1] *Understanding Human Nature*, 1927.

of the struggle, for it is presupposed in the struggle, nor can it come out of the nature of the individual, for what he feels himself to be and what he really is, is a failure. Does not this point to a source outside?' [1]

(*d*) Another theory is that the dynamic which produces the great religious experience is a principle of human nature working towards equilibrium and tranquillity of soul. This was best expounded by Jung, who, more than Freud or Adler, took a genuine interest in the subject of conversion. On this view the *fons et origo* is a principle which does for the mind what the *vis medicatrix*, as it used to be called, does for the body in mobilising the forces that fight a disease, and building it up in health and strength. When the soul is torn by conflict the mind has a natural tendency to seek to bring about a settlement, and also the means at its disposal for effecting it. A chief cause of the spiritual conflict is that men fall into two main classes: the introverts, who chiefly cultivate the inner life, and the extraverts, who chiefly live and have their being in the external world; and as this one-sidedness entails much misfit with the world and with fellow-creatures, the beneficent principle comes into play with a view to effect some combination of the conflicting attitudes. And so conversion is described as the process whereby the mind of the introvert is directed outward to service and the mind of the extravert is directed inward to the things of the spirit.[2] The urge to equilibrium is also regarded as fundamental by Tansley, who

---

[1] Hughes, *The New Theology and Religious Experience*, p. 234.
[2] Jung, *Psychological Types*, 1926, pp. 412 ff.

specified three ways in which peace is compassed: the inhibition of one of the conflicting forces, the entertainment of a delusion, and the relegation of painful experiences to the unconscious.[1]

That a harmonising urge is at work in the mind is not open to doubt. The mind as well as the body is the seat of a principle that makes for health and peace. But it may not be thought that the soul is in a better state than the body that is assailed by diseases with which the defensive and restorative principle proves unable to cope. The mind can do something to check the progress of its dangerous diseases, and more to persuade itself that they are non-existent or not serious, but to affirm that its power is equal to mastering the disease of sin, and producing a new creature of the quality amounting to a true conversion, is in flagrant contradiction, not only with the considered testimony of the Christian Church, but with the most patent facts of human nature.

3. According to a second school, religious experience is pathological. The forms in which piety has risen above the commonplace have even been diagnosed as deep-dyed with insanity. This standpoint may be illustrated from a book in which Dr. Adler deals with the content and the formation of character.[2] The convert figures among the portraits of the four temperaments. Of these the sanguine type is his favourite; he alone has the title to be called a good man, though it does not

---

[1] *The New Psychology*, 'The Equilibrium of the Mind,' pp. 59 ff.
[2] *Understanding Human Nature*, 1927, p. 263.

appear that religion counts for much, if anything, in his spiritual make-up. It is the melancholic type—the man of the gloomy countenance who habitually looks on the dark side of things—that is taken as the representative of religion. He is a person who has got into difficulties 'with the absolute truth and logic of common life'—which means that he has failed in most things that he has tried, and is ever bewailing his ill-fortune, though he also feels some pride in being singled out for such exceptional treatment. He often beats a retreat into religion, for he deems himself the object of a divine chastening, and hopes that God may do him good after He has done him much evil. He sorrows much over his sins, stares into the past and wastes his time in fruitless introspection, until in his vanity he seeks to transfer his burden to a complacent God—'believing as he does that this revered Being is concerned entirely with him and has nothing else to do but occupy Himself with his troubles.' Dr. Adler doubtless met with cases of this kind in his practice. But it is expected of those who make scientific generalisations that they have first made a study of all the relevant facts, and there is much more to be said about repentance and faith than the psychiatrist has discovered in the dwarfed or disordered minds of certain patients. Had he acquainted himself with the results of American research, he would have known that those who have passed through the experience of mourning for their sins have ordinarily looked back on it as a salutary stage in their spiritual history, that issued in a new character and a new

life in which they possessed God, without dreaming
that they had a monopoly of His favour, got rid of
their self-centredness and their vanity, and devoted
themselves to the service of God in the service of
their fellow-creatures. Nor has the judgment of this
school on the saint been more flattering than that
on the convert. A prevalent estimate is that the
roots of sainthood are to be found in a frustrated
sexuality; and attempts have been made to demon-
strate that those whom the Church has revered as its
greatest saints were actually insane.

4. The average teaching of the New Psychology is
that religion formerly served a useful purpose by
bridling the instincts and helping to make the human
situation bearable, but just as this was effected by
faith in an imaginary divine being or beings, religious
experience has decayed as the result of enlightenment, and is doomed to disappear; and that from
the evolutionary point of view it may not be doubted
that religion has existed because it is of some advantage in the struggle for existence. 'The dynamic
value of religious belief,' says Leuba, 'must be
reckoned among the mighty influences contributing
to the development of the human race.'[1] Belief in
powerful mysterious beings, good and evil, stirred
the imagination, stimulated the rational powers, and
summoned forth the hidden potencies of the mind.
Moreover, as gods were made the embodiment of
the ideals of a community, religion exercised a
powerful moralising influence. That religion is
nevertheless an evanescent phenomenon of human

[1] *A Psychological Study of Religion* (French Trans., 1914), p. 14.

history is maintained on the ground that there is no rational basis for faith in God, and that it is steadily declining on the higher levels of intelligence, and in proportion to the spread of scientific culture. And Leuba is confident that adequate substitutes will be found; as the work of religion was done, not by divinities that were the object of faith, but by the powers of the human mind which religious faith brought into play.[1]

The distinctive service of Christianity, Jung explains, was to liberate souls from a painful anxiety-complex, 'by an exercise of psychologic projection.' It might be sought to get rid of the complex by suppressing and forgetting all about a disturbing element, but even when one is thus freed of conscious conflict 'it lies invisible at one's feet and is stumbled over at every step." 'The religious projection offers much more effectual help, as it keeps the conflict in sight, and gives it over to a divine personality standing outside of oneself.' 'Just as psychoanalysis in the hands of the physician, a secular method, sets up the real object of transference as the one to take over the conflicts of the oppressed and to solve them, so the Christian religion sets up the Saviour, considered as real, in whom we have redemption through His blood, the forgiveness of sins.' [2] It was indeed a serious weakness that, in the psychologist's view, the object to which the burden was transferred was unreal, but as Christianity also required men to bear one another's burdens, it thus made some provision

---

[1] *Op. cit.*, chap. xiii.
[2] *Psychology of the Unconscious*, 1922, pp. 39 ff.

for transference to a real object. And this Christian technique had astounding success in defending the ancient world against 'the demons that harbour in the human soul' and the 'whirlwinds of the unchained libido.' If in our time religion has fallen into the background, one reason is that we have ceased to realise the tremendous and unabated power of original sin, and do not know how much Christianity formerly did to counteract the sinister forces in human nature. At the same time, Jung is of opinion that the biological utility of the Christian religion has ceased inasmuch as it helped human thought to attain the independence in which it dispensed with God, and is now impotent because its theological assumptions have become unbelievable.[1] Tansley also gives a sympathetic description of religious procedure with a like forecast. 'The most permanently successful of the protective devices,' he says, 'are those which project the ideal unification of the mind into a supernatural sphere, where it is safe from direct attack. . . . This safeguarding of the ideal, eventually hedged about with all the authority of a great organisation, the Church, has resulted in the relative permanence of a high standard of life and conduct which has been of incalculable service to mankind. But the results of even this great and sustained effort at unification fail to resist the assaults of rational scepticism and the slow sapping effect of objective knowledge.'[2]

It is a fair judgment on this contribution to causal explanation that it has brought out that the instincts

[1] Op. cit., p. 45.   [2] The New Psychology, p. 291.

are a more influential factor in the general religious life than had been realised, but that the work done by them as a whole, and by any one of them singly, has been greatly exaggerated. Their rôle is not that of a leader in the work of conversion, but of auxiliaries that are pressed into the service.

That the instincts named make their influence felt in the religious life, and indeed render an important service, has always been recognised to some extent by Christian thinkers. A favourite argument of some defenders of the faith has been that the Christian salvation shows so marvellous an adaptation to the capacities and needs of human nature as to justify the inference that it proceeded from Him who as the Creator of men knew what was in man. And one illustration is that Christianity is strikingly adapted to enlist the support of the instincts, self-regarding and earth-bound though they are, in persuading the natural man to make the great spiritual adventure of a new life. This is illustrated by the three instincts of which so much has been made by recent psychologists. But the contention that any one of them, or all of them together, is the primary agent in the conversion of souls is shown to be untenable by a variety of considerations. One is that there is an objective factor in the form of a gospel which has a much stronger claim to be called the principal cause. Human nature is the same always and everywhere, but conversions have not occurred always and everywhere, only in periods and in societies in which there was being proclaimed a gospel or an ideal calling to a higher life, from which it is rightly inferred that the instincts cannot of themselves effect the change, but at the most do something to persuade a person to give the thing a trial. Another consideration is that conversions take place in a being who has not only instincts which he shares with the animals but a religious and moral nature, and it must be attributed in no small degree to these that he can behave very differently from a mere animal. A third observation is that, while the instincts may be brought to acquiesce in and even support the spiritual adventure because of something in it that appeals to them, their interests are so entirely different that they are incapable of initiating it and carrying out the experiment. For Paul's word holds: 'I find a law in my members warring against the law of my mind, and it holds me captive.'

Accordingly, the genetic explanation of religious experience which finds the primary causal factor in one or more of the instincts underestimates when it does not ignore other factors, notably the higher strain in human nature and the gospels and ideals provided by prophetic religions, while it greatly exaggerates the work done by the instincts in the religious field. The religious function attributable to the instincts is limited to the fact that their support can be enlisted for a gospel or an ideal to some extent inasmuch as these contain offers and promises cognate with, though far transcending, the ends for which they work. That they were incapable of initiating and carrying through the experience of true conversion is proved by the fact that such only recur in societies which possess an awakening gospel or an inspiring ideal or a gospel which enshrines an ideal. Nor may it be said that the instincts account for the experience of the prophetic teachers who gave gospels and ideals to the world, for their distinction from the common herd was that in them the divine strain in humanity predominated.

The conflict among estimates of the psychological schools lends support to the view that the science of psychology as such is not qualified to assess the value of religion, and that it ought to remit the question to a higher court. The applied science of psychiatry has an interest in the bearing of personal religion, or the want of it, on mental and bodily health, but a psychiatrist may not go on to assume, as he is tempted to do, that the supreme value is physical health, and that all over-values, including the religious and the ethical, fall to be measured by the criterion of biological utility. It should be obvious that it does not fall within the scope of a department of natural science, even if its subject-matter be mental, to assess the comparative importance of the values which have emerged in the history of mankind. This task falls to philosophy as the science of sciences.

The result of the psychological inquest into religion has been to offer a choice between two differing valuations. The depreciatory and contemptuous estimate is based on an investigation of the extremely varied phenomena in which attention was chiefly given to morbid or degenerate types. The moderate and complimentary estimate does more justice to the facts, but it is quite illegitimately coupled with an assumption that the religious experience has no objective counterpart in a higher world; and also takes for granted, in spite of the spiritual law of the ebb and flow of faith, that an indifferent and agnostic mood of the last two generations represents the final attitude of civilised humanity to God and divine things. Science has certainly not disposed of the conviction that there is an experience of union and communion with God that is the supreme human privilege, that a genuine conversion is the most salutary event that can occur in the history of a soul, and that true sanctity is the most sublime and beautiful of all forms of spiritual attainment.

V

DIVINE CAUSALITY

In view of new light from psychology on the proximate causes of religious phenomena, the question was revived as to whether and how far divine causality enters into the process. The general view, endorsed by an international conference of psychologists, was that the science should confine its attention to the causal factors of the natural order and not take sides in regard to the questions of supernatural agency and the first cause. 'Religious psychology,' Ribot observed, 'can progress only by avoiding, and referring to philosophy, the insidious questions in which it stands in danger of being entangled.' [1] There were, however, those who held that the scientific findings justified and even demanded a metaphysical venture.

[1] *Archives de Psychologie*, II.

On one view it is at least a probable opinion that the religious phenomena pointed to an influx of light from a higher source. 'Much new light,' wrote William James, 'has been thrown on the conversion experience in the scientific investigation, especially by the discovery of the activities of the sub-conscious,' and as a psychologist he added, 'I do not see why the reference of the phenomenon to a subliminal self should exclude the notion of the direct presence of the Deity, and of a higher penetration.' 'But just as our primary wide-awake consciousness throws open our senses to the touch of things material, so it is logically conceivable that *if there be* higher spiritual agencies that can directly touch us, the psychological condition of their doing so *might be* our possession of a subconscious region which alone should yield access to them. The hubbub of the waking life might close a door which in the dreamy Subliminal might remain ajar or open.' 'At the stage of solution or salvation a man becomes conscious that the higher part of him is conterminous with a *more* of the same quality which is operative in the universe outside of him, and which he can keep in working touch with, and in a fashion get on board with and save himself when all his lower being has gone to pieces in the wreck.' 'The conscious person is continuous with a wider self through which saving experience is literally and objectively true as far as it goes. . . . And the natural appellation for this higher part of the universe, the supreme reality, is God.' [1]

[1] *Varieties of Religious Experiences*, 1903, pp. 242, 508, 515, 516. (Published by Messrs. Longmans, Green and Co., and quoted by kind permission of Mr. Henry James.)

Much commoner is the opinion that the outcome of the investigation has been to show that there is no supernatural factor in religious experience. 'We may set it down,' says Leuba, 'that it is made up of the same elements as the rest of conscious life, and elaborated according to laws holding for mental life generally.' [1] When miracles in the physical world became unbelievable, Hoffding remarks, many still clung to a belief in miracles of the inner life, but these also have been discredited.[2] The temple has at last been inspected by competent observers, and they found that its Holy of Holies contains nothing save some gifts of the worshippers. But has this really been proved?

For nearly two thousand years there has existed an institution, including most of the intellectual power as well as of the piety of the Western world, which sincerely taught, and persuaded the nations to believe, that the piety and the virtues of truly good men and women are due to a divine influence described as the work of God, or of the Holy Spirit. And there were felt to be strong reasons for holding and proclaiming this doctrine. It was not merely that it was taught in the New Testament, and that in particular the Apostle Paul, speaking for the believer, testified— 'By the grace of God I am what I am.' This alone is not sufficient to explain the belief, for in decadent periods the tendency has been to minimise and even to ignore the dependence of the spiritual life on the initiative and the support of heavenly grace. There were in addition two compelling reasons which led

---

[1] Leuba, *op. cit.*, pp. 288, 289. [2] *Philosophy of Religion*, 1906, p. 102.

M

the Church, or at least its higher mind, to confess
that the spiritual life and power of the faithful were
derived from a divine source. One was that those
who had undergone a true conversion had normally
a strong and ineradicable conviction that they had
been apprehended by God, and that it was likewise
due to His help that they progressed in the divine
life and persevered therein to the end. The other
was that, when men reflected on the radical change
that had taken place in their thoughts, their feelings
and their volitions, it seemed clear that they had not
in themselves the inclination or the power to bring
it about, and that it could only have been wrought
by Him with whom all things are possible. And these
grounds are still sufficient to support belief in a divine
causality in the conversion and sanctification of souls,
and the more so that the new Psychology agrees in
substance with the doctrine of original sin.

It is argued, as by Leuba, that while there is a
possibility that there is a God who influences human
souls, there is no evidence of it. But the fact is that
we have precisely the kind of evidence that was to
be expected if the ultimate reality is a personal being
who enters into communion with human creatures
made in His image. Religious experience is akin to
the relationship between an obedient child and a
good father, or between a docile disciple and a
revered teacher, and, as in the human parallel, it is
natural that a chief impression made on the mind of
the beneficiary should be a sense of indebtedness to
the benefactor and of the magnitude of the debt.
Moreover, as the relationship between God and the

finite soul is closer than the most intimate of human intercourse, it was to be expected that the soul that has been thus visited and blessed from on High should obtain the irresistible conviction to which theology has attached cardinal importance as the inner witness or the testimony of the Holy Ghost.

The ground on which psychologists have denied the presence and work of God in the soul is that there is much in religious experience which has been traced to secondary causes, and that some addition has been made to our knowledge of these by recent investigation. But even if it could be shown that all that occurs in religious experience is traceable to secondary causes, it might still be held that the second causes point to a first Cause, and that as the Creator of the instrumental means, God is still to be regarded as the author of the spiritual experience. For a theist, God is at least the ultimate benefactor, and the only question is whether our debt to Him is limited to what was done in the making of man and the establishment of spiritual laws, or whether this has been supplemented by an immediate and supernatural influence which He exercises upon the souls that He has made and that He has so wondrously endowed. In the former case we think of the work of God in the human realm as analogous to that of the head of a great business which is carried on under rigid rules, and it is surely the worthier conception that there is in addition an aspect of the works of God corresponding to the life of home and friendship, in which the animating principle is love, and actions are not bound by rules and benefactions proportional to deserts. Accordingly, once and again, as against Pelagianism and theological Rationalism, the Church has declared that grace is more than the provision for spiritual well-being that was inserted into the ordered scheme of things, and that in the greatest experience of the spiritual realm the decisive factor is an immediate gift from the Lord and Giver of Life.

Chapter VIII

THE RECENT SITUATION

A HUNDRED years ago Christianity seemed to be firmly established as the spiritual director of the higher civilisation. The Roman Catholic Church had emerged with unabated strength from the upheaval of the French Revolution and the subsequent conflicts. The Protestant Churches possessed an evangelical tradition, confirmed by Wesleyan and kindred revivals, which had enriched their membership with decided Christian personalities, made of the typical family an efficient school of spiritual training, and left a deep impression on the character of great nations. In the following decades there was a series of movements, with the significance of an experiment in the laboratory of history, which tested the vitality of the Christian Church, the efficacy of its message and its methods, and the value of its religious and moral products. One result was the formation of a large and ever-growing mass of paganism within the bounds of Christendom. The other was a vigorous reaction of Christianity to the menace in the way of defensive and offensive measures. In a brief review of the latter-day crisis we shall touch on the strength and the weakness of the pagan revival, the qualified success of the Churches in their capital task of the conservation and reproduction of a higher

181

humanity, and the Christian counter-attack in the form of special missions for the recovery of the lost ground.

During the last three generations many influences have concurred to impede and thwart the work of the Church as the school of Christian character. It was a period of boundless material progress, though it is a commonplace that human talent has hitherto been much more evident in the production of wealth than in the management of its resources. And the economic conditions of the period had serious consequences for the spiritual life. The general mind became decidedly secular, as the growing power of man over nature gave promise of the attainment on earth of a degree of the felicity which the fathers had only expected in a future life. From a spiritual point of view the economic development proved a severe ordeal both for the successful and the unsuccessful. The capable and ambitious had unusual opportunities of acquiring wealth and all that it purchases, but in so doing were in danger of thinking that the supreme rule of life is the gospel of getting on, and of making a god, if not of Mammon, at least of the self which Mammon does so much to gratify and exalt. The working classes generally had much material profit from the industrial revolution, but much deterioration followed on the migration of large bodies of the population to new homes in strange surroundings and their detachment from the restraining and guiding influences of the settled community. More grievous was the trial and the tribulation of the multitude which earned by its unskilled labour the bare means of subsistence, and which lived under the conditions of the congested area and the one-roomed house in which it was difficult to preserve the vision of God and divine things, and to observe the elementary laws of decency and morality. In some quarters the growing indifference of the masses to religion was changed into hostility. English Chartism had at least a vein of militant atheism, and on the Continent Karl Marx had much success in persuading the proletariat to despise religion as an opiate, and to declare war on the Church as the confederate of the ruling class in the oppression and exploitation of the toiling millions.

The period also began with a passion for liberty in the many senses of the word, but it was found difficult to combine them in a working programme, and latterly there has been a growing disposition to subordinate the other forms to the ideal of national autonomy and power. One form is personal liberty, which has been approved in a high sense by the moralists who have proposed self-realisation as man's chief end, but in popular circles it has been widely interpreted as the right to do what is pleasing in one's own sight without regard to the authority of the moral law, and with a special dispensation in favour of the lusts of the flesh. Not least was it a period in which the intellectual genius of the race continued its triumphant course in the extension of our knowledge of the realms of nature, of its contents and its laws, its genesis and its development. The impression made on many who have shared in this work, and proclaimed to the people as a finding of science, is that the discoveries have discredited the Christian view of human history as a meeting-place of the natural and the supernatural, and at the most have left it possible to believe in an infinite Power which is the ground and source of all that has been, is, and will be, but whose nature is unknown and unknowable. And without doubt this negative attitude has a far-reaching influence on the cultured and half-cultured classes. There is a section which openly declares its rejection of the essence of the Christian faith; another keeps silence, whether because it knows of no working substitute or dislikes to speak of such things; while many do not themselves know whether or how much they continue to believe.

The contemporary world has reproduced not a few of the features of the Graeco-Roman world at the beginning of our era. Now as then there has been a far-reaching movement of religious unsettlement and moral disintegration, accompanied by a feeling that mankind has lost its way, and also by attempts to find substitutes for a traditional religion believed to be outgrown. As in the days of the Roman Empire, there is an opinion that the needs of the multitude are satisfactorily met by the provision of bread and games, for it might seem that its chief interest, when it has been relieved of anxiety about the daily bread, is in the contests of men, horses and dogs which are witnessed by spectators on the spot, or reproduced at the fireside with the help of the newspaper or the broadcasting apparatus. A larger class than of old is now in a position to make its chief end the pursuit of pleasure, but in doing so only repeats the discovery that peace of mind is not found by hastening

from place to place, even when the speed has been
vastly accelerated by the express, the motor-car and
the aeroplane, and that the harvest to be expected
from the dissolute career may still be summed up in
the worm, the canker and the grief. In the ancient
period, again, the world was given a new object of
faith and worship by the deification of the Roman
Emperor, and the modern counterpart is reverence
for a nation as the divinest object within our ken, and
the exaltation above the measure of humanity of the
leader who symbolises its ideals and furthers its interests.
Again, some of the Caesars took the view that the
Church was a negligible quantity, others that it was a
serious danger to the commonwealth, and the modern
parallel is that, while most modern States decided to
terminate the alliance with the Church as unprofitable,
the latest rulers of Russia have attempted to destroy
it by a combination of violence and ridicule. The
body of professing or virtual pagans in our midst, no
doubt, shares in the virtues of the Greeks and Romans.
One section consists of men whose master-passion is
the love of truth and the desire to spread the light,
and another of men of action who rejoice to be alive
in a world in which there are big things to be done,
and who when they succeed in winning great prizes
become examples of liberality and munificence. A
further parallel is that there has been a recrudescence
of types of thought which gave guidance and comfort
to distracted souls in the Graeco-Roman age. As then
some turned to mysterious Oriental cults, so now
some have discerned a city of refuge in spiritualism
or theosophy. In the circles in which the Christian

view of God and the world has been found unbelievable many of the noblest spirits have followed the
lead of the Stoics, and decided that the best that can
be made of the human situation is to recognise the
reign of law in the universe, to take for guiding-star a
lofty ethical moral ideal, to endure in patience, and
to help others to endure.

II

Throughout this turbulent and dangerous period
the capital task of the Church was the shepherding of
the many millions who had been born into the household of faith. And in this work it has had, along with
a distressing measure of failure, a more than respectable measure of success. No doubt it has fallen
far short of its professed purpose of remaking its
members in righteousness and holiness after the likeness of Christ. If its work be compared with that of
a factory, it must be confessed that a large proportion
of its products seem to be worthless, the great bulk far
below standard, and the best with serious blemishes.
But it is still a marvel, and a beneficent marvel, that
the vast majority of the population of Europe voluntarily belongs to an institution whose programme is to
make men and women good according to the mind
of Christ and to carry on the unselfish and gracious
work that was instituted by His ministry. It has also
to be taken into account that, disappointing as are
the results of the work of the Church, there is no
substitute for it as a school of character, and also that
it has to be judged by what it has prevented as well
as by what it has accomplished.

The Roman Catholic Church has on the whole held its own with its remarkable combination of earthly and heavenly gifts. With its age-long experience it has a profound knowledge of human nature, it has extraordinary business capacity with a talent for statecraft, and this equipment has been invaluable in organising the work of the institution with wise regard to the principle of the division of labour, and ensuring that it rested on a sound financial basis. There has been a providential check on its worldly efforts in that its grandiose schemes in the political sphere have usually failed, and that in those periods and countries in which it has reached the heights of power and wealth it has suffered its greatest losses and humiliations. On the other hand, it is foolish as well as uncharitable to be blind to the divine side of its mission, and the notable outcome of its world-wide and intensive spiritual labours. It possesses remarkable influence over a vast multitude of persons on the lowest social and intellectual plane, and has persuaded them that man has the stated duty of worshipping God, and ought to live a decent and moral life. Another feature is that, commonplace as may be the religion and morality of the general body, the Roman Catholic Church has elicited, and continues to elicit, from the élite of its membership an extraordinary response to the call for sacrifice in the form of ready obedience to orders and of gratuitous or ill-paid services.

The Eastern Orthodox Church had a similar record down to recent times, and if in the cataclysm which has overtaken it we may discern a judgment on it

for its superstition and its servility to a tyrannical
State, there is good reason to hope that the indubitable saintly core of that great historic communion
will survive as gold tried in the fire, and prove the
nucleus of another holy Russia with a better title to
the name.

The Protestant Church has less claim than the
Roman Catholic Church to political talent and
business capacity. Apart from considerations of
Christian duty, it was the height of unwisdom that,
instead of seeking to maintain a united front, it
quickly broke up into the two sections of Lutheran
and Reformed, while during the next three centuries
the Reformed section continued to subdivide on issues
which ought to have ranked as secondary. From the
business point of view the shortcomings were that it
very imperfectly realised the need of a division of
labour in order to increase efficiency, and that in its
zeal it ever tended to exceed its visible resources and
to accumulate deficits on its schemes. As a school of
religious and moral character the Protestant communions have done a work of cardinal importance
for the higher life of a great mass of the population
of the countries in which they predominate. Every
national Church of the Protestant family has
produced, and continues to produce, a distinctive
type of character which in its genuine representatives
has enriched the moral life of society, and made a
real addition to the salt of the earth. The marks of
the Lutheran type have been depth of religious feeling,
a faith in the gospel of the assured forgiveness of sins,
and the conception of the Christian life as a state of

spiritual liberty realised in willing obedience to the
law of Christ. The Anglican type has been distinguished by loyalty to the faith once delivered to the
saints and entrusted to the guardianship of the
Church, a deep reverence, a joy in the outward
expression of the beauty of holiness, and a sane balance
of judgment in the adjustment of the claims of the
sacred and the secular domains. The 'Reformed'
type, strictly so-called, has been criticised as Judaistic,
philistine, pharisaic, though with the admission that
the Calvinist was an extremely efficient citizen whose
industry was very profitable to the commonwealth
and who, in doing well for himself, brought much
gain to others, and was an important factor in the
growth of the wealth of nations. No doubt there
were tyrants and hypocrites among them : self was
very painfully prominent in many who were un-
doubtedly God-fearing and high-principled, and the
lives even of the best were not conspicuously adorned
by the graces of the Sermon on the Mount. The
following may be quoted as a fair estimate of the
excellences of the type as produced from generation
to generation in the Church of Scotland : 'This is
the general picture of them as I have known them—
diligent in business, truthful in word, upright in deed,
cautious and moderate in judgment though with a
reserve power of dogged determination and moral
indignation, clean in heart and mind, loyal to friends
and to principles, reticent in religion but possessed
withal by a deep fear of God, by a deep reverence
for holy things, by a warm attachment to the Church
visible, and by a courageous faith in the gospel of

Christ and the life of the world to come. We have also had our special type of womanhood, which at its best had hardly its equal in intellectual vigour, and certainly not its superior in unselfish and self-sacrificing devotion.'[1]

The lesser Protestant sects have chiefly impressed critical outsiders by peculiarities which they summed up as narrow-mindedness and self-righteousness, but on a closer inspection it appears that every considerable denomination which has survived in the spiritual struggle for existence has stood for a principle that deserved recognition, and has had a soul of true religion and sound morality.

When we compare the success of the Catholic and Protestant divisions of the Church in the production of a new humanity, it would appear that each has had the better results in particular fields, and that each has something to learn from the other. A central feature of the message of the Reformation was the assertion of the priesthood of all believers, and the profit of the doctrine was that a large section of the membership reached a high level of Christian zeal and endeavour. One result, specially conspicuous from time to time within the Presbyterian Church, was that the husband and father took very seriously the position of priest in the family, and that there were innumerable homes that had the character of a forecourt of the temple as well as of an effective school of Christian culture. A second result was that in the more radical section of Protestantism the laity were given a real share in the government of the Church, and that the educational and philanthropic service

[1] W. P. Paterson, *In the Day of the Ordeal*, p. 145.

of the clergy was supplemented by the labours of a host of Sunday School teachers, district visitors and other contributors to the life and work of the Christian congregation. It has been, and still is, no small part of the strength of Protestantism that it possesses, especially in the great cities, many congregations which provide a true fellowship in a Christian atmosphere, stir the imagination with heavenly visions, and develop Christian character in the support of Christlike works, ranging from the conversion of the heathen to the brightening of the lives of the boys and girls of an adjacent slum. The Protestant Churches, as becomes more and more evident, have not been equally successful in convincing the mass of a professedly Protestant population that it is a duty and privilege to attend Church on Sundays, that they may be edified by the reading and preaching of the Scriptures and join in the prayers in which due homage is rendered to God and supplication made for His forgiving, enlightening and ennobling grace. From the influence of the Roman Catholic Church in this regard, the moral may be drawn that in order to grip and sway the multitude in religion a Church must strongly assert, and from the heart believe, that it has the support of divine authority, and that there is much gain to the soul from the worship of the sanctuary.

III

The rise of a non-Christian population within the borders of Christendom made it urgent to supplement the pastoral work of the Churches by missionary efforts aiming at definite conversions. The Roman Catholic Church has faced the task, and with considerable results among lapsed and indifferent Protestants, though the gains have probably been at least counterbalanced by its own losses from similar causes, while in Catholic countries particular classes and interests have hardened into declared hostility. Certainly no recent Catholic missions to the godless masses have been comparable in popular appeal to the medieval missions of Franciscan and Dominican friars.

The Lutheran Church has shown little evangelistic zeal, as this was held to be out of place in ordinary worship, and of lesser value for those outside the fold than the witness of Christian character and the works of the Good Samaritan. In the Reformed Church it was usual, in the distinctively evangelical periods, for the preacher to divide the congregation into the classes of the converted and the unconverted, and to call upon the unregenerate to repent and believe the Gospel. The Church of Scotland was deeply stirred in the eighteenth century by religious mass-meetings leading to some notable revivals, and during the latter half of the nineteenth century there was warm support in evangelical circles for similar efforts. The United States, with its Puritan tradition and its heterogeneous population of diverse origins, has naturally been a sphere of evangelistic effort, and from Jonathan Edwards to D. L. Moody the Protestant Gospel, though with diminishing stress on the terrors of the Lord, was proved to be the power of God in the conversion of sinners. According to American reports, however, the revival meeting on old lines has become less and less effective, and the chief reliance is now placed on the work of the ordinary ministry, and the contagion of Christian conviction and devotion.

In view of the spiritual condition of the contemporary world the call to evangelistic effort is unescapable, and in the recent period there has been a series of missions to special classes which have had striking success in producing a change of character and life. The Salvation Army was formed to attack the lowest social stratum, in which Christianity had almost been suppressed, and it achieved extraordinary results on a world-wide scale by preaching the traditional Protestant Gospel, of ruin, redemption and regeneration, in a setting of human sympathy and of efforts for social betterment. The Student Christian Movement had a similar response from a cultured class to a message which was substantially a reproduction of the Galilean Gospel, with its special emphasis on the privileges of following Christ as a leader in the greatest of conceivable ventures. More recently the Oxford Group Movement, specially directed to spiritual derelicts of the higher social class, has achieved remarkable results in Europe, Africa and America by the proclamation of a Gospel which substantially reproduces in a setting of Christian fellowship the call to repentance and faith in Christ which produced so remarkable results in the apostolic and sub-apostolic age. Finally, there is the movement led by Karl Barth, with its imperious summons to bow before God in lowly reverence and obedience,

N

and which, if so far it has chiefly produced a second conversion in the class of ministers and students, also gives promise of becoming an evangelistic force in the life of nations. It has to be added that these movements were initiated and inspired by individuals who had to create their own sphere of influence, but when their power and value had been demonstrated they were approved and supported, or imitated, by the ecclesiastical.

There was nothing new in the modern counter-attacks on lapsed or lapsing masses within the Christian pale. The message of the Salvation Army was the Gospel according to Luther; of Barthianism, the Gospel according to Calvin; while the Student Christian Movement and the Oxford Group Movement recalled the simpler formulation of the Gospel in the teaching of Jesus and the apostles. The success was largely due to the fact that the Good News was a novelty to persons who had not known, or had never seriously considered, the Christian way of deliverance from the evils which burdened and darkened their souls. Moreover, each of the missions owed much to impressive leadership, which was supplemented in three of the movements by membership in a quickening and protecting fellowship. Their influence has, however, been restricted, either intentionally or in fact, to particular classes, and there has been no stirring of the general mind and conscience on a scale remotely approaching the spiritual upheaval of the Reformation, or the evangelical revival of the late eighteenth and early nineteenth centuries. It may be that the work

will extend in the form of an aggregation of missions
that will concentrate on other social or cultured strata
and emphasise those aspects of the Gospel which are
best fitted to satisfy special needs and aspirations.
But it may also happen that the sectional mission
will expand into, or be cramped by, a general mission
which, transcending the differences of class culture
and environment, will address man in his generic
character of a creature bearing the divine image
polluted and enslaved by sin, and invite him to use the
means of salvation which are provided in the gospel
of the grace of God. The urgency for an evangelistic
effort of the widest scope was recently emphasised
by the Archbishop of Canterbury in an address in
which, after a glance at the growing paganism of
the Continent, he warned our people to remember the
beam in its own eye—the drift away from religion
under the influence of a secular civilisation, which
crowds God out when it does not openly deny Him—
and called upon the faithful laity to co-operate with
the clergy in a recall to religion.

In the year after the war the Church of Scotland
carried on a mission with a similar call to re-dedica-
tion, and ten years later a second was organised under
the guidance of Dr. Donald Fraser, a former leader
in the Student Christian Movement, which sought to
move the nation as well as the Church by a re-
proclamation of the gospel of the Kingdom of God.

The Faith and Order group, and the Life and Work
group, have been working for a united front in
opposition to the forces making for religious backsliding and apostasy, and for a common understanding

N I

as to the content of the Gospel which it is the privilege of the Churches to proclaim. There is, therefore, a call to ponder anew the spiritual needs of the natural man, the provision made in the many-sided Christian Gospel for meeting these needs, and the means of persuading sinners of mankind to repent and believe in the Saviour, and to obey in newness of life. The natural condition of mankind is, without doubt, a state of grievous spiritual distress. It is true that in the general opinion it is good to be alive, and this is confirmed by the observation that for every new generation life is an extremely interesting adventure, and that at a later stage the abounding labours and sorrows are mixed with joys, while familiarity can make painful afflictions tolerable, and reconcile to the most sordid occupations and surroundings. The spiritual distress is due to the fact that man is the cleverest of living creatures, and is also endowed with a moral and religious nature. The situation is bewildering, for human life is a riddle which baffles common sense and for which obviously an agreed solution has not been found by the wisdom of this world. It is alarming, for if there be no God, the individual is at the mercy of blind forces which gradually sap his strength and eventually destroy him, and as a sinner he is liable, if there be a God, to punishment in this life, with the menace of fuller retribution in a future state of existence. It is a disappointing existence, for men are strongly impelled to the selfish pursuit of gain and pleasure, and yet when most successful are fated to discover that there is a hunger which can only be satisfied by bread from heaven. Finally, it is a humiliating situation, for, as a being of a higher order, man acknowledges the obligation to obey a self-denying law of duty, while yet he confesses that he does the evil that he would not, and is unable to do the good that he would.

It is written that Jesus knew what is in man, and the Gospel was proposed as a remedy for each of these palpable ills. It replaces the bewilderment by the assurance that God did not leave us to guess and speculate about the deepest questions of existence, but that He Himself has instructed us, and that by the mouth of the prophets, and lastly through the teaching, the person and the life of His Son, He gave us surely to know Himself, and His holy and loving purposes concerning man. The danger from the side of an offended God is averted by the promise of the forgiveness of sins on gracious terms, and the danger from the destroying forces of nature by the assurance that he who possesses the friendship of a heavenly Father who possesses the powers of the Omnipotent Ruler has nothing to fear from the grim possibilities of this world or the next. The unrest of the earth-bound spirit, it is further promised, may be replaced by a peace of mind which the world may disturb but which it cannot take away. Last but not least, it is provided that the humiliating sense of moral weakness will be dispelled by the gift of the Holy Spirit whereby the penitent and believing soul receives supplies of life and light and power from the inexhaustible fountain above.

In view of the fact that the sense of need varies in

kind and degree in different quarters, it was proper
that the missions directed to particular classes should
have in view the outstanding need of those addressed,
and emphasise the provision made for it in the Gospel.
In the circles permeated by scientific culture, and by
the preponderantly godless spirit of recent literature,
it may be felt that the chief misfortune of our time is
ignorance of truths which it is of vital interest to
know, and that the greatest service that can be
rendered to the doubting and disbelieving is to
persuade them to trust Christ as the revealer of the
nature and purposes of the Supreme Being. In the
circles dominated by worldliness there is a widespread
sense of the emptiness and bitterness in which the
self-seeking life eventually issues, and the one thing
needful may seem to be to proclaim that the soul
has no rest until it finds rest in God and in the following of Him who was meek and lowly in heart. There
is also a class, largely represented among the youth
of every generation, which is ready to respond to a
call which lifts it out of the ruts of the customary and
the commonplace, and to this class is profitably
addressed the call to accept the self-sacrificing ideal
which was set forth in the teaching and made beautiful
by the example of Jesus Christ. It has, however,
never been more than a small minority which has
felt that the worst of its evils was agony of doubt, or
unrest of soul, or the lack of a compelling idea. The
antecedent and deeper evil is alienation from God,
of which the penalty is the lack of the inspiration,
guidance and comfort that are received through
communion with Him of whom and through whom

and to whom are all things. The primary purpose of the Gospel, therefore, is to give the sinner to know God and to settle him in right relations with God, so that his soul may be disburdened by the forgiveness of his sins, and his life enriched by all that involved the friendship of a reconciled Father in Heaven. For the evangelistic mission of the Church the fundamental problem is how the careless and indifferent mass is to be quickened to realize the existence of God, to be persuaded to seek His favour and help as their chiefest privilege, and give to Him the central place in their lives. The Gospel, we believe, is from God, but men have to be moved to accept it and act upon it, and to this end it must be presented in a form that wins the support of elemental principles of human nature. And it may be said that the essence of a successful evangelistic technique is that the Gospel should be so presented as to take captive certain instincts which powerfully affect human conduct, and to enlist them in the highest service of the soul.

It is an important factor in the persuasive power of the Gospel that it promises through the friendship of God the satisfaction of the instinct which aims at the preservation and the signal enrichment of our existence. The main reason why Christianity was welcomed by the ancient world and taken over by the youthful peoples of the West was that it had the character of a great salvation which credibly offered to men a divine protection against the wasting and destroying forces of time, and also an enduring possession of all good things worthy to be included in the inheritance of the sons of God.

In the great religious revivals of the past, both Catholic and Protestant, the capital theme ever was the blessings and the conditions of the Christian salvation. As a fact the natural man is ever asking 'Who will show us any good?' and may be persuaded to join in the prayer, 'Lord, lift Thou up the light of Thy countenance upon us.' If another religious revival is to be seen on a large scale, it will be brought about, not by a call to live up to an ideal, and do something for the advancement of the Kingdom of God, but by the promise in the name of God of the victory over death, and the gift in this life of an instalment of the best of the blessings that it has entered into the heart of man to conceive.

The message which drew men to God by the attraction of a great salvation had its natural complement in a warning as to what they had to fear if they should miss or forfeit it. Much was made of the terrors of the Lord, both by Jesus and the apostles; the Roman Catholic Church still has the courage to declare that the wicked shall be turned into Hell, while all but the saintliest Christians have to look forward to the torments of Purgatory; and in the earlier period Protestant Churches deepened the gloom by reducing the possibilities to a Heaven for which the fewest seemed to be prepared and a Hell of unspeakable and everlasting torments. And doubtless one of the chief causes of the general drift from religion in Protestant lands is that there has come to be little of the old belief in a wrath of God which punishes in this life by special judgment, and which will be fully manifested at the end of the world. It is of course true, as the author of Job protested, and our Lord repeated, that particular calamities may not have the character of judgments, and the current doctrine of Hell was offensively materialistic as well as unduly dogmatic in regard to its duration. Yet on Christian premises the unreconciled sinner has much reason to be afraid, and to be without godly fear is evidence of blindness rather than of heroism. There is reason to fear the ruthlessness of the forces of the natural order if we have not the protection of Him who is the Lord of nature, and also the retribution to be expected from the God whose love is certainly not to be resolved into irresponsible good nature. If we believe in the God of the Christian revelation we shall at least recognise some events in our own lives as judgments upon our evil deeds or wandering ways. If we believe in a future life we are bound to believe that there is some future punishment in store, whatever the form out of which it will be executed, which shall be commensurate with the heinousness of unforgiven sins, and appropriate to the character in which the fruits of a sinful life are preserved. It was therefore out of Catholic wisdom, as well as loyalty to a doctrine closely bound up with the faith, that the Archbishop cited the warning of the prophet—'if thou do at all forget the Lord thy God I testify against you that ye shall surely perish.'

The Gospel also makes a strong appeal to the instinct to which psychology has given the name of tender emotion. In the human sphere this instinct takes many forms, among them the love of man and woman, parental affection, friendship, devotion to a leader, local and national patriotism; and the Gospel proposes as the supreme object of human love the all-perfect Being, almighty, all-wise and all-good, to whom we owe our existence and all that it contains of worth and beauty, and who is able and willing to enrich us further beyond all that we can ask. And as it is difficult for our weak minds to realise the invisible God, and to cleave to Him as a reality, we are given to see Him as God manifest in Jesus Christ, whom to know as He laboured and suffered out of love to man is to be constrained to love in return. In the latest phase of popular evangelism, as represented by D. L. Moody, the emphasis was shifted from the wrath of God to the unspeakable love of God which moved Him to give up His Son to death for the sake of His enemies, and the appeal was summarised in the exhortation provided by the Fourth Gospel to love Him because He first loved us. In the latter days, indeed, the doctrine of the love of God has seemed to be discredited by our wider knowledge of the world order, which has more resemblance to the organisation of a factory than to the life of a home, but there is still enough to reassure us if we apply the criterion that a giver is known by his gifts. For the best explanation of the fact that man feels the spell of lofty ideals, and that such an one as the selfless and sinless Christ appeared among men, is that the infinite Being who is the source of all created life is a God whose crowning attributes are holiness and love.

An evangelistic mission addressed to man as man need not offer much formal defence of the faith.

Christianity is best defended by explaining the benefits which the Gospel offers to man, and the terms on which they are offered. It is, however, indispensable that the message should be proclaimed with authority as proceeding from God Himself, and also that the messengers should bespeak assent and trust because the Gospel manifestly burns as a fire in their bones and sets their souls aflame. It will probably also be found that if the multitude is to be interested, it must be moved by the recognition of utter self-sacrifice on its behalf, which might point to the creation of a Protestant order of evangelists who should take temporary vows of poverty, celibacy and unquestioning obedience. Modern psychology may not admit a religious instinct, but in man as we know him there is at least the capacity of recognising the divine when it comes impressively within his ken, and the impulse to render it due homage, and this inward corroboration has been abundantly in evidence whenever God has been made known in His perfections, and especially when the Christ has been preached in whom God and His saving purpose were revealed.

In every generation since the coming of Christ there have been those who repented and believed the Gospel, and became in a true sense new creatures. The converted, however, were never more than a minority, in some periods a small minority, of the multitude to whom the Gospel was preached, and it was a problem why the same means should be efficacious for the saving of some, while the many were left untouched and were even hardened. It has been held in the Augustinian and Calvinistic schools, with support from St. Paul, that the decisive factor is a divine influence which makes the call effectual in the case of elect souls, and that where this is wanting the Good News falls on deaf ears. The tenet of the effectual calling of favoured persons was eventually rejected by the Lutheran and Anglican Churches, and it was repudiated by Wesley and Booth as implying that while the Gospel was to be preached to all it was only possible for some to accept it. It is now a prevalent view in all branches of the Church that the factor which determines the result is the self-determined will of the individual, who has at least the power of resisting the call to repentance, but it still needs to be explained why some, who equally with the others are corrupted and enslaved by sin, should alone be able to accept the invitation to put off the old man with his deeds, and to enter on a new life bearing the yoke of Christ. Doubtless it would be unwise to load and prejudice the evangelistic message by a doctrine of election, but it must nevertheless be granted that such as have experienced a radical conversion have good reason to think that all of it was God's doing, including the will to believe and obey, and that they are entitled to believe that He who began the good work in them will ensure that they persevere to the end.

It is also a mystery that, while human nature remains unchanged, the Gospel so signally suited to its needs has been much more welcome and efficacious in some periods than in others. Nations and groups of nations have been stirred to feel that religion was the one thing needful, and thereafter

have fallen away into formalism, indifference and
scepticism.   The spirit of the recent period has been
growingly secular, and the causes which have excited
popular interest and enthusiasm have been chiefly
bound up with political and social interests.   There
have, however, been recent movements, as we have
seen, that have evoked a widespread interest in a
saving message, and given to many the experience of
a new birth.   Are these occurrences to be thought
of as the beauties of a sunset or as the shafts of light
that pierce the darkness and herald the dawn of
another day?   That they are of the sunrise, not of
the sunset, is to be believed on two grounds.   One is
the promise of times of refreshing from the presence
of the Lord; the other is that it is a lesson of history
that the ebb of spiritual life is followed by a turn of
the tide.   The paganising movement of the Renaissance was overwhelmed by the spiritual fervour of
the Reformation, the worldliness and the unbelief
of the eighteenth century were shamed and checked
by a far-reaching evangelical revival, and there is
reason to hope for another baptism with the Holy
Ghost and with fire which will revive the sense of
God, and the felt need of God, enthrone the Saviour
in penitent and believing hearts, and also awaken a
zeal for some palpable form of self-denying service of
God.   History repeats itself, but always with a difference, and it may be that in the next revival the passion
engendered by a new-born faith will have a character
of its own.   In the Middle Ages it seemed to many
that no cause was so sacred as the recovery of the holy
sepulchre from the infidel; in the Reformation and

post-Reformation epoch many godly men felt that their chief privilege was to slay or to be slain in a holy cause; while the zeal of others went chiefly into polemics. Since the evangelical revival, many of the noblest spirits have felt, and with good warrant in Scripture, that the greatest of Christian privileges is to sacrifice self in obedience to the command—'go ye into all the world and preach the gospel to every creature.' Defenders of the faith will continue to be honoured and the missionary passion will be re-inforced by every religious revival, but it may be that the distinctive feature of the next revival will be the baptism of Christian masses with the spirit of brotherly love, so that it will become for many a second nature to follow the example of Him who cared not for Himself but was in the world as one that served. And since with God all things are possible, it may even happen, at least for a season, that the heart of the nations will be changed so that they will begin to love one another, and to do to others as they would that others should do to them.

INDEX